THE GREATEST MEN OF THE BIBLE

CLARENCE MACARTNEY

The GREATEST MEN OF THE BIBLE

Abingdon / Nashville

THE GREATEST MEN OF THE BIBLE

Copyright © 1941 by Whitmore & Stone

Abingdon Reprint Library Edition 1980

All rights reserved.
No part of this book may be reproduced in any manner whatsoever without written permission of the publisher except brief quotations embodied in critical articles or reviews. For information address Abingdon, Nashville, Tennessee.

ISBN 0-687-15780-3

Manufactured by the Parthenon Press at
Nashville, Tennessee, United States of America

FOREWORD

Some years ago I set aside a space in the weekly bulletin of the First Presbyterian Church and invited the members of the congregation to vote for "The Ten Greatest Men in the Bible." When a sufficiently large poll had been secured, I announced the ten who received the highest vote, and some months afterwards preached a series on these ten characters of the Bible. There were really eleven of them, because Samuel and John the Baptist were tied for tenth place.

In this book the first eleven sermons deal with the eleven characters who stood highest in the vote; and in order to make the volume complete, and include all the great men of the Bible, I have added four others. I think it can be said that this list is a fair representation of the major characters of the Bible.

Early in my first pastorate, at the First Presbyterian Church, Paterson, New Jersey, I made the important homiletic discovery that the people like to hear sermons on Bible characters, and that the preacher can preach on Bible characters more naturally, fluently, and practically than on any other subject.

I recall what I heard a man of taste and distinction once say about his minister, who was an able man and preached carefully prepared sermons. This member of his congregation went regularly to church and waited faithfully on the preaching, the merit of which he freely acknowledged. But he said he would have much preferred that his minister, instead of laboring to be profound, or quoting other writers or speakers, or commenting on national and international affairs, had taken the old stories and the old characters of the Bible, and with that for a start drawn some wholesome and timely lesson.

It is not possible to preach on the great men of the Bible without speaking practical and timely truths to the people, and in a way that everyone will understand. The great advantage of such preaching is that you summon these men themselves into the pulpit and permit them to preach for you. Abraham preaches on Faith; Elijah on Righteousness; Samuel on Judgment to come; David on Temptation; and Peter on Repentance. Every chord in the great harp of the Gospel is struck by the preacher who preaches on the great men of the Bible.

But what about the women of the Bible? I have had frequent requests for sermons on the great women of the Bible. On many of them I have already preached, and at some time in the future I hope to preach a series of sermons which will take in all the notable women of the Old Testament and the New Testament.

CLARENCE EDWARD MACARTNEY.

CONTENTS

                              PAGE

I
PAUL—MORE THAN CONQUEROR 9

II
DAVID—THE MAN AFTER AND AGAINST GOD'S HEART 26

III
MOSES—THE MAN OF THREE MOUNTAINS . . 41

IV
JOHN—THAT DISCIPLE WHOM JESUS LOVED . 56

V
PETER—THE MAN WHO WAS SAVED BY A LOOK 69

VI
ABRAHAM—THE MAN WHO PASSED THROUGH THE GREATEST TRIAL 84

VII
JOSEPH—DREAMS, DUNGEONS, DIADEMS . . . 98

VIII
ISAIAH—THE MAN WHO SAW CHRIST'S GLORY . 113

IX
ELIJAH—THE SON OF THUNDER 128

X
SAMUEL—THE MAN WHO PREACHED FROM THE GRAVE 143

XI
JOHN THE BAPTIST—THE FRIEND OF THE BRIDEGROOM 158

XII
JEREMIAH—THE MAN WHO LOOKED LIKE CHRIST 174

XIII
DANIEL—THE MAN WHO LIVES FOREVER BECAUSE HE SAID NO 186

XIV
JOSHUA—THE MAN AFTER WHOM JESUS WAS NAMED 198

XV
JOB—THE MAN WHO MADE SATAN QUIT . . 208

I
PAUL—MORE THAN CONQUEROR

> "Nay, in all these things we are more than conquerors, through him that loved us."
> ROMANS 8:37

WHEN LORD NELSON REPORTED TO THE BRITISH Admiralty his great victory over the French fleet in the Battle of the Nile, he said that Victory was not a large enough word to describe what had taken place. When Paul spoke of the victory which, through Jesus Christ, he had won over all the ills and adversaries and temptations and woes of life, that greatest of all words, conqueror, was not sufficient to describe it; and therefore he said, "More than conquerors." "Nay, in all these things we are more than conquerors, through him that loved us."

"More than conqueror." That is the only phrase which seems adequate when we come to speak of Paul. Paul was always a struggler and a battler—always a warrior, a contender, contending against the Christian disciples when he persecuted them, battling with Jews, battling with Gentiles, battling with Roman officials, battling with Jewish ecclesiastics, battling with mobs, battling with false friends, battling with weariness and fatigue, battling with thorns in the flesh, and, finally, battling with death itself. Yet in all these things he was more than conqueror.

On one occasion, after he had been delivered out of great peril at Ephesus, where he had the sentence of death passed on him, and after he had been delivered out of deep and painful anxiety concerning the church at Corinth by the return of his messenger, Titus, Paul cried out in the joy of his soul, "Thanks be unto God, which always causeth us to have a triumph in Christ!" There he made use of the greatest of all Roman scenes and pageants, a Roman triumph. The Triumphal Arch was the last word in Roman art and splendor. With their sculptured reliefs depicting battles and sieges in all parts of the world, these great arches, such as that of Titus and Constantine, look grandly down today upon the heap of rubbish and the sea of ruins that once were Rome. Bitten and defaced by the winds and rains of ages, scarred and battered by catapult and cannon, these arches have survived the vicissitudes of centuries.

Before the Triumphal Arch came the Triumphal Procession. Sometimes, as in the case of Julius Caesar, these great spectacles of victory came after a long lapse of years, when peace had been established. Arrayed in silken garments and crowned with garlands, the conqueror rode in his chariot at the head of his victorious legions. At the wheel of his chariot walked the princes and potentates who had been taken captive, and who, after having helped to make a Roman holiday, would be strangled or decapitated in prison. As the procession moved toward the walls of the city along the Appian Way, or the Via Sacra, successive pageants and pantomimes recalled the incidents of the conqueror's battles and campaigns, while clouds of incense went up to heaven from the altars which had been reared along the line of march. It was this greatest of Roman scenes and exhibitions which Paul had in mind when he employed it as a metaphor to describe the triumph he had won through faith in Christ. Always he is the triumphant man, "the more than conqueror."

How shall we speak of such a man as this? Of all the great men of the Bible, Paul is the most difficult to preach on—not because of any moral lapse in his life which must be explained or excused, as in the case of some of the other great men, and not because of the lack of knowledge concerning him, for we know more of him, what he thought, what he felt, what he aspired to, and what he suffered than we do of any other man in the Bible. It is for that very reason, that we know so much about him, and because he is great however you take him, great as a thinker, great as a preacher, great as a friend, great as a builder and planter, great as a sufferer, and great in his world-embracing love, that it is so difficult to speak of him. On what side shall we start to climb this mountain? It would take the golden measuring rod of the Angel of the Apocalypse to measure Paul. It would take the sevenfold chorus of the Archangels to sound his praise.

I

PAUL IS THE GREATEST PROOF OF THE RESURRECTION OF CHRIST AND OF THE TRUTH AND POWER OF THE GOSPEL

To understand how that is, you must remember, first of all, who this man was that was converted to Christ there at the gates of Damascus. He was not a stranger who had never heard of the claims of Christ. He was not a man who was indifferent to Christ and who did not care whether he was an impostor or the Messiah of Israel. Neither was he just an ordinary enemy of Christ. He was Christ's fiercest foe, "an Hebrew of the Hebrews," trained in all the traditions of Israel, a graduate of the School of Gamaliel, passionately devoted to the hopes and revelations of Israel. His whole nature revolted in anger and disgust at the claim of these mendicant preachers that the Galilean peasant who had been crucified between two thieves had risen from the dead, that he was the Messiah of Israel, and that through faith in him the world had eternal life.

With all the terrible intensity of his nature Paul took upon himself the office of chief persecutor of this despicable heresy. He himself tells us that he was exceedingly "mad" against the church and persecuted the Way unto the death; and his biographer, Luke, can only say of him that he "breathed out threatening and slaughter against the disciples of the Lord." When Stephen was stoned, his murderers laid their garments at the feet of Saul, and with the joy of the fanatic he saw the cruel stones reach their mark.

Such was the man who was on his way to Damascus to persecute and slaughter the Christians there, when he saw a light and heard a voice. "Saul, Saul, why persecutest thou me?" Three days after that, this fierce foe of Christ is proclaiming him as the Messiah and the Saviour of the world! With amazement, and with joy, the Christian disciples heard that "he which persecuted us in times past, now preacheth the faith which once he destroyed." "And they glorified God in me," Paul himself reports. And the whole Church of Christ, ever since, with those first disciples, has glorified God in the conversion of Paul.

The means of Paul's conversion was as remarkable as the conversion itself. All men are converted by the influence of God's Holy Spirit, but here is a man who was converted through a special resurrection appearance of Christ. In his other appearances after his resurrection Christ had showed himself alive by infallible proofs to his disciples. Those appearances were not to convert his enemies, but to confirm and establish the faith of his disciples. But here it was different. Christ appears in person to Saul of Tarsus and says to him, "Why persecutest thou me?" This is why Paul in his great chapter in First Corinthians on the resurrection of Christ and the immortality of the soul, after he has cited the different appearances of Christ, how he was seen of Peter, and of the Twelve, and of five hundred of the brethren, and then of James, and then of all the apostles, says, "last of all he was seen of me also, as of one born out of due time." It was that appearance which changed the cruel and persecuting enemy of Christ into his greatest friend, and changed, too, the history of the world.

The results of Paul's conversion are not less remarkable than the conversion itself or the means by which it was effected. The bitterest foe became the greatest friend; the blasphemer became the preacher of Christ's love; the hand that wrote the indictment of the disciples of Christ when he brought them before the magistrates and into prison now penned the epistles of God's redeeming love; the heart that once beat with joy when Stephen sank beneath the bloody stones now rejoiced in scourgings and stonings for the sake of Christ. From this erstwhile enemy, persecutor, and blasphemer came the greater part of the New Testament, the noblest statements of Christian theology, the sweetest lyrics of Christian love, the most saintly and heroic personality who has ever borne the name of Christ.

This is why Paul in his conversion, in his Christian ministry, in his Christian life, is the greatest witness to the resurrection of Christ and the power of the Gospel. If you are ever tempted to ask, Is Christ real? Is Christ historic? Is the Gospel true? Then remember Paul, who he was, and what he became. Remember that Saul of Tarsus became Paul the Apostle!

II

PAUL IS THE GREATEST EXAMPLE OF THE CHRISTIAN LIFE

If there was never such a conversion as that of Paul, neither has there ever been such a Christian. The first thing that strikes one about the Christian life of Paul is his magnificent thought of man. The moment we pronounce that name, Paul, then man, in spite of his fall, in spite of his weaknesses, in spite of his corruption, is crowned with honor and dignity. When we think of Paul, we cry out with the Psalmist, "Thou hast made him a little lower than the angels, and hast crowned him with glory and honor."

Paul was ever jealous of his own rights as a man; and although he was always ready to be all things to all men, he resented to the utmost personal injustice. Witness his rebuke of the High Priest who commanded him to be smitten at his hearing before the Sanhedrin: "Sittest thou to judge me after the law, and commandest me to be smitten contrary to the law? God shall smite thee, thou whited wall!" Witness what he said to the Roman officers who had unlawfully scourged him at Philippi, and then, discovering that he was a Roman citizen, begged him to withdraw quietly from the city. Paul answered, "They have beaten us openly uncondemned, being Romans, and have cast us into prison; and now do they thrust us out privily? Nay, verily; but let them come themselves, and fetch us out." Magnificent self-respect! And no man will revere and respect others who does not first of all respect himself.

Sometimes the minister will get discouraged when he learns of unworthy conduct and life on the part of those to whom he ministers. But think of Paul! He speaks to thieves and drunkards, and adulterers, and tells them to sin no more. He tells them that they are "called to be saints," that they have been called to "honor and glory and immortality."

With that high Christian thought of man as a child of God and a candidate for honor, glory, and immortality, there went a corresponding love for man.

PAUL—MORE THAN CONQUEROR

The greatest tribute ever paid Paul was that by the golden-mouthed preacher of Antioch, John Chrysostom. In his "Homily on the Letter of Paul to the Romans," Chrysostom says that he loves Rome most of all cities because there Paul died, and there he will be raised up to meet the Lord in the air. He says he would like "to see the dust of Paul's body that sowed the Gospel everywhere, the dust of that mouth which lifted the Truth on high, and through which Christ spake great and secret things and greater than his own person; the dust of those hands off which the serpent fell into the fire, and through which the sacred writings were written; the dust of those feet which ran throughout the world and were not weary; the dust of those eyes which were blinded gloriously, but which recovered their sight again for the salvation of the world; the dust of that heart which a man would not do wrong to call the heart of the world, so enlarged that it could take in cities and nations and peoples; which burned at each one that was lost, which despised both death and hell, and yet was broken down by a brother's tears."

Paul was worthy of that high tribute, "the heart of the world." One night in his dream at Troas he saw a man from Macedonia standing over against him, who said, "Come over and help us." Henceforth Paul, wherever he goes, to Philippi, to Athens, to Corinth, to Rome, is on the search for the man from Macedonia. Sometimes that man is a Jew, sometimes a Gentile, sometimes a Greek, sometimes a barbarian, sometimes free, sometimes a slave; but always Paul is on the search for him and ready to help him. The desperate tide of the whole world's anguish was forced through the channels of Paul's heart. "Who," he cried, "is weak, and I am not weak? Who is made to stumble, and I burn not?" He lived and toiled as a man who was debtor both to the Greek and the barbarian. Wherever a man breathed, wherever a soul was enshrined, there was Paul with his burning earnestness and his yearning love.

Another remarkable thing in Paul's Christian life was his courage, his fortitude and endurance. Once when the veteran Macedonian soldiers of Alexander the Great threatened to mutiny, and charged him with being indifferent to their hardships and wounds, Alexander sprang up on the dais and said to his soldiers: "Come now, who of you has wounds, let him bare himself and show them and I will show mine. No member of my body is without its wounds. I have been wounded by the sword, by the arrow from the bow, by the missile from the catapult, I have been pelted with stones and pounded with clubs while leading you to victory and to glory."

Paul, a greater conqueror than Alexander the Great, could say that too. He could say, and did

PAUL—MORE THAN CONQUEROR

say, "I bear about in my body the marks of the Lord Jesus." What a catalogue of woes he mentions! His stripes above measure; his prisons more frequent; of the Jews five times, forty stripes save one; thrice beaten with rods; once stoned; thrice shipwrecked; in journeyings often; in perils of waters; in perils of robbers; in perils by his own countrymen; in perils by the heathen; in perils in the city; in perils in the wilderness; in perils in the sea; in perils among false brethren; in weariness and painfulness, in watchings often, in hunger and thirst, in fastings often, in cold and nakedness. What a catalogue of woes! And all this he endured with a thorn in the flesh which would put the ordinary man in a home for incurables. Heroic battler, noble wrestler for Christ! Was there a peril of sky, or sea, or earth thou didst not face? Was there a cup of bitterness thou didst not taste? Was there a thorn to which the flesh is heir that did not pierce thee? Yet, through it all, Paul was more than conqueror! Let those who think they are handicapped by some affliction in body or in spirit for a noble work in life remember Paul. One has said,

"Milton the blind, who looked on Paradise!
Beethoven, deaf, who heard vast harmonies!
Byron, the lame, who climbed toward Alpine skies!
Who pleads a handicap, remembering these?"[1]

[1] Violet Alleyn Storey, in *Tea in an Old House*.

But if these, Milton and the rest of them, stir us to endurance and achievement, what shall we say of great Paul, who marches on from year to year, from sea to sea, from nation to nation, from victory to victory, till from the gates of death we hear his final cry of triumph, "I have fought a good fight, I have finished my course, I have kept the faith: henceforth, for me a crown."

III

PAUL THE GREATEST PROCLAIMER OF THE CROSS OF CHRIST

Paul was "bought with a price"; and henceforth his mission was to tell the greatness of that price, the exceeding greatness of it, even the Precious Blood of Christ. That was the truth which he said always, "first of all," he declared unto men, "that Christ died for our sins according to the scriptures."

This was natural and inevitable; for the Cross of Christ had saved him, the chief of sinners, and thus made him an example to all ages of the power of Christ to save. Paul is not content with being the great example of conversion and redemption; but, inspired by the Holy Spirit, he proclaims the way of Salvation. He can tell it in a single sentence to the anxious jailer who says to him at midnight, while the dust is still rising from the fallen walls of the prison,

"What shall I do to be saved?" "Believe on the Lord Jesus Christ and thou shalt be saved." But he can also proclaim it in words of incomparable splendor and power, taking in the whole history of the Plan of Resurrection, from the time it was a mystery hid with God from before the foundations of the world, until that day when it shall have reached its grand consummation and the last sinner shall have been brought home to God and God shall be all and in all. Sometimes he plunges into deeps that are too deep for us, and sometimes he rises to third heavens into which we cannot follow him; but always there is the beating heart, always a personal relationship to his Saviour, of whom he says, "He loved me and gave himself for me." He will not glory in anything save in the Cross of the Lord Jesus Christ. "God forbid that I should glory, save in the cross of our Lord Jesus Christ." As the greatest representative of the power of the Cross to save, he is also the greatest proclaimer of the Cross, the ambassador of Christ who beseeches men to be reconciled to God. And most wonderful of all, this mighty soul, this "more than conqueror," who endured such woes and sorrows, who spake such wondrous words, who accomplished such great things—this man invites us, invites you and me, to follow him, even as he followed Christ! All that Christ did for him, Paul declares he can do for you and me. When we think of that, what can we do but cry out with Paul himself, when he thought of what God had done for him, "O the depth of the riches both of the wisdom and knowledge of God; how unsearchable are his judgments, and his ways past finding out!"

Unworthy though I was, I found myself in the King's Country. After the sorrow and strife and gloom and discord of earth, how bright and fair and tranquil seemed this heavenly land. When I had recovered from my first transport of joy, and was able to think again, I remembered some of those great souls of the Bible, and how I had hoped that one day I might see them in Heaven and talk with them. Meeting one of the great angels, I said to him, "Where shall I find Abraham, the Friend of God, for I wish to ask him about that sacrifice of Isaac on Mount Moriah?" Answering me, the angel said, pointing to a great avenue, "Take yonder Highway of the Nations and follow it till you come to the Sea of Glass mingled with Fire; then turn to the right until you come to the River of Water of Life; follow it until you come to Mount Zion; and on the other side of the Mount you will come to the Throne of the Lamb, and just near the Throne of the Lamb, in the Inner Circle, you will find Abraham."

I thanked him, and then said to him, "Where will I find Joseph? I would like to talk with him." To my surprise he gave me the same directions which he had given for finding Abraham. Then I asked for Moses, for I wanted to talk with him about Mount Pisgah; and Samuel, for I wanted to talk with him about Saul; and Elijah, for I wanted to ask him about what he said to Christ on the Mount of Transfiguration; and David, for I wanted to ask him about the Psalms; and Isaiah, for I wanted to ask him about the fifty-third chapter of his prophecy; and John the Baptist; and John the Divine; and Peter, for I wanted to ask him about that special and private appearance of Christ to him after the Resurrection. To my great surprise the angel gave me in every instance the same direction he had given to find Abraham.

I thanked him and started on my way. Presently I came to the Highway of the Nations, and at once I began to understand the meaning of that great passage of John, how he said, "They shall bring the glory and the honor of the nations into it." Here so often what we see is the shame and the sorrow and crime and dishonor of the nations; but there I saw the glory and the honor of the nations—Israel, Egypt, Babylon, Assyria, Greece, Rome, Spain, Russia, Germany, Britain, and America. Following the Highway of the Nations, I came at length to the Sea of Glass mingled with Fire; and there the sight was so beautiful, and the music of the harpers harping with their harps so entrancing, that I well nigh forgot whither I was going. But when the music ceased for a moment, I remembered and went on my way, till presently I came to the River of Water of Life. There, too, I fain would have remained and rested under the shade of the Tree of Life and listened to the gentle laving of the River of Water of Life. But pressing on, I saw before me Mount Zion; and passing over it I came at length to what I was sure must be the Throne of the Lamb, for there was a rainbow of strange and overwhelming glory hovering round about the Throne.

Here in front of the Throne, and in the Inner Circle, just as the angel had told me, I found Abraham, and Joseph, and Moses, and Samuel, and Elijah, and David, and Isaiah, and John the Baptist, and John the Divine, and Peter. They were all listening with rapt and eager countenance to one who was speaking to them as he stood there between them and the Throne of the Lamb. I wondered at first if I could understand what he was saying, or if the language of Heaven would be strange to me. But as I drew nearer, I heard familiar words, for it was Paul who was speaking. He told again the story of that day at Damascus when Christ appeared to him. I heard him pronounce again that beautiful lyric of Christian love, "Now abideth faith, hope, charity, these three; but the greatest of these is charity." I heard him say again, "This is a faithful saying, and worthy of all acceptation, that Jesus Christ came into the world to save sinners; of whom I am chief." I heard him say again, "God forbid that I should glory, save in the Cross of our Lord Jesus Christ." I heard him say again those words, which more than any other that he wrote and spoke explain the grandeur of his life, "I live by the faith of the Son of God, who loved me, and gave himself for me." At that, Abraham, Joseph, Moses, Samuel, Elijah, David, Isaiah, John the Baptist, John the Divine, and Peter sprang to their feet, and with David the sweet singer of Israel leading them, and all heaven, angels and archangels, and all the blood-washed company of the redeemed joining in the song, they sang together, "Unto him that loved us, and washed us from our sins in his own blood, and hath made us kings and priests unto God and his Father."

With the burst of that triumphant song I awoke, and lo, it was a dream! But a dream which by God's grace, I hope will one day come true. Will you, too, be there to sing with Paul and Moses, and David, and Isaiah, and John, and Peter, and all the redeemed of God, that Song of Redemption? Can you say now, "I live by the faith of the Son of God, who loved me, and gave himself for me"?

II
DAVID—THE MAN AFTER AND AGAINST GOD'S HEART

> "I have found David the son of Jesse, a man after mine own heart."
> ACTS 13:22
>
> "But the thing that David had done displeased the Lord."
> II SAMUEL 11:27

A MAN ONCE WROTE ME AFTER HEARING A SERMON on David, and asked me, "Why do you think so much of David?" and then went on to enumerate some of David's gross transgressions. Perhaps the best answer would be, "Because God thought much of him."

We read in the First Book of Samuel that "all Israel and Judah loved David." Apparently, Israel and Judah still love him, for in the vote of the congregation on "The Greatest Men of the Bible," David comes second, next to Paul. Everybody loved him. Whether it was Samuel, or Saul, or Jonathan, or Bath-sheba, or Abigail, or King Hiram, they all loved him. There is something in David that makes the heart leap. His very name sets all the chords of life to vibrating with sweet melody.

Whose are the faces that you would like to see first of all in heaven? Each man for himself; but I will tell you those whom I would like to see first

DAVID—AFTER AND AGAINST GOD'S HEART

of all. First, it would be that face that was marred for me on the Cross, the face of him who died for me, and in which is reflected all the love and all the pity and glory of God. Then, I would like to see the face of Paul. Great Paul! He would make a heaven all by himself. But after Paul, the next one for whom I would look would be David, and I am sure it would be difficult to get a glimpse of David because of the crowd that would always be pressing about him.

David was a great sinner; but we love him in spite of his sins, and because in his sins, he so greatly repented and was forgiven and forever teaches transgressors God's ways. We do not love David because he was a cruel murderer and adulterer, but because his nature was generous, open, kind, magnanimous, devotional, reverent, thankful and in his deep sin, he repented and was forgiven.

I

DAVID AS A MAN AFTER GOD'S HEART

That description of David is often wondered at and sometimes scoffed at. How could you call an adulterer, a murderer, a man who practiced great cruelty, a man after God's heart? But this was spoken of David, let it be remembered, in contrast with Saul, and before he was made king; and once again, long after David's death, it was spoken of him in contrast with Jeroboam, the king who made Israel to sin. The sins of David are always denounced and unsparingly punished; yet, even so, there was much in David that was after God's heart, so many beautiful traits that it is well for us to think upon them and to endeavor to imitate them.

David was the most thankful man of the Old Testament, as Paul was the most thankful man of the New Testament. In everything David gave thanks and called on all creation, animate and inanimate, winds, seas, mountains, stars, clouds, cedars of Lebanon, beasts, men and angels, to praise God. The universe was not big enough for David when his heart was filled with praise and thanksgiving. We can be sure that God loves the thankful man. Isaak Walton said of David in his *Compleat Angler*: "Let me tell you, and though the prophet David was guilty of murder and adultery, and many other of the most deadly sins, yet he was said to be a man after God's own heart, because he abounded more with thankfulness than any other that is mentioned in holy scripture, as may appear in his book of Psalms; where there is such a commixture of his confessing of his sins and unworthiness, and such thankfulness for God's pardon and mercies, as did make him to be accounted, even by God himself, to be a man after his own heart."

DAVID—AFTER AND AGAINST GOD'S HEART

Another reason why David was a man after God's heart was because he was a man who loved God's cause in the world. There was no doubt about that. His heart was never weaned away from God's kingdom, even in the hour of his sin and fall. It was David who planned, although he was not permitted to build, the Temple.

David was also a man of filial piety. That is always the mark of a good man. In one of the darkest hours of David's life, when he was hunted by his enemies, we find him turning aside to take thought for his mother and father and convey them to a place of safety.

David was a magnanimous man. Twice when he had his great enemy Saul in his hand he spared him. He practiced forgiveness and loved his enemy long before David's Son stood on the Mount near the Sea of Galilee and pronounced his sublime Beatitudes and taught men the beauty of forgiveness.

David had a great heart—and it's the heart, aye, that makes us right or wrong. Chrysostom called Paul the heart of the world. One might well call David the heart of mankind. The measure of his heart is the Book of Psalms. There is a legend that David, sleeping once at night on the roof of his palace, heard the wind sweeping through the wires of his harp and making beautiful melody, arose from his couch and taking his harp sang the words and music that he had heard. Here in this harp of the Psalms is sounded every note of man's heart—the joy of being, the delight of God's House, the hope of future glory, the witness of past ages, the coming of the kingdom. And here also we hear the minor chords struck, the sick man's groan, the prisoner's sigh, the penitent's prayers, the despair of the oppressed, the sinner's moan, the song of forgiveness and the confidence of the dying. The music of David fits itself into all the circumstances of the soul. With David's words we enter God's House, with David's words we utter the deep desire of the soul, with David's words we go down into the River of Death. His Shepherd's Psalm—"The Lord Is My Shepherd I Shall Not Want"—after the words of Jesus himself, "Let not your heart be troubled: ye believe in God, believe also in me," has helped more souls over the River, I suppose, than any other part of the Bible. It will do for us when we are little children, and as yet know nothing of "death's dark vale" or the stain of sin. It will do for us in the midst of life's strength and years; and when the noise of life is passing and the earth recedes, it is the music of that psalm that will go with us over the River into the King's country.

II

DAVID AS A MAN AGAINST GOD'S HEART

We have spoken of David as a man *after* God's heart. Now let us look at him as a man *against* God's heart. And is there anything strange in that? What is that but the eternal duality of man's nature? Do we not all discover within ourselves that man who is after God's heart, and also another man who is against God's heart? Paul himself discovered within his own breast those two warring and irreconcilable men—the man after God's heart and the man against God's heart. He said: "I delight in the law of God after the inward man: but I see another law in my members, warring against the law of my mind and bringing me into captivity to the law of sin which is in my members." David himself could have written that.

The Bible paints men just as they are. We are glad that the Bible did not leave out this dark story of David's transgression and sin. In his reverent commentary on the fifty-first psalm, Augustine, who himself was also a man both after and against God's heart, expresses his regret that in explaining the psalm it was necessary for him to recount the sin of David whose repentance gave utterance to the psalm. "But," he says, "God would not have hushed what he hath willed to be written." More than anything in the Bible, perhaps, the fall of David teaches us the awfulness of sin and the certainty of punishment, and warns us how even a good man, a man who talks of God and worships God, and serves him and praises him and prays to him, can fall into the pit of transgression and sin.

David's temptation and sin is an old, old story, and yet one that is ever new. It is a timely theme today, when it is frequently broadly intimated that higher pleasures are to be found in the indulgence in sin, and in sin of this kind, whereas always, within and without, there is no sin which so blasts and scars and stains the human soul.

David fell in an idle moment. He ought to have been at the wars, at the front, instead of idling at home. Long after David's sin and fall, James related the history of it, and the history, too, of every other similar transgression, when he said: "Every man is tempted, when he is drawn away of his own lust, and enticed. Then when lust hath conceived, it bringeth forth sin: and sin, when it is finished, bringeth forth death." His sin illustrates, too, the terrific injury that can be wrought to a soul in a moment of time. In a moment of time, in an "only-this-once," lasting and eternal good can be done to a soul; but alas! also, in a moment of time, in a moment's acquiescence, in a moment's glance, in a moment's decision, terrific damage can be done to a man's soul.

The worst thing about David's sin was the cruelty and treachery with which he tried to cover it up. He is an absolute monarch, yet he knows that the thing which he has done is wrong, that it has displeased God, and he tries to hide it from man. Through his cruel device the husband of the woman with whom he has sinned is killed in war, fighting in the forefront of the hottest battle, giving his life for his king and country, and yet being treacherously slain, because, at David's direction, Joab has left him alone in the post of danger. Then, David, deceiving himself into thinking that all was well, married Bath-sheba. "But," it is written, "the thing which David had done displeased the Lord." Oh, that eternal, irrevocable, unbending, inexorable, unprofitable *"but"* of conscience, when conscience says to us, "The thing which thou hast done displeases God."

III

DAVID'S CONVICTION AND REPENTANCE

God waited long for David to repent. I cannot think that during this period, between the consummation of his crime, and the coming of Nathan, David could have been happy. Sin, indeed, has terrible powers of deception, and nothing so blinds us to our sin as the fact that it is ours. Nevertheless, I cannot believe that David, with the history that he had back of him, was a happy man during this period. Too many hours of fellowship with God, too many plans for his Temple, too many holy aspirations, too many psalms and songs indited, for David to feel comfortable after that sin. I imagine, too, that not a few of the angels when they heard of David's fall, took their harps and hung them on the branches of the Tree of Life on the banks of the River of Life, unable now to sound the praises of heaven because David, the best representative of their harmony and symphony on earth, had fallen from the favor of God. There must have been times when he could have wished that his eyes had been blinded before he had taken that fatal look on the housetop that led to his sin. But regret is not repentance. Regret can pass and fade, and still the soul go unchanged.

Then God sent the prophet Nathan. What a preacher Nathan was! How courageous, for he was talking to a king who had the power of life and death in his hands, and how faithful to the Word of God, and how tender and true! Nathan was an old friend of David, and it is often easier to speak to a stranger than it is to a friend about God. Nathan had planned together with David for the building of the Temple, and the two men, no doubt, had sweet conversations. But now he must go and point out David's sin. Nathan might have openly named the sin of David, and denounced him as the sinner, and pronounced judgment upon him; but instead of that he chose the far better way of describing David's sin and then letting David pronounce judgment upon himself. So skillfully did Nathan state this hypothetical, imaginary case of the poor man who had that little ewe lamb with which his children played, which drank of his own cup and lay in his bosom, and how the rich man who had exceeding many flocks and herds, when a traveler came to visit him spared of his own flock and took the poor man's lamb and dressed it for the man that was come unto him—so skillfully did Nathan tell that story that he almost overdid it. David's anger was aroused, and laying his hand on the hilt of his sword, he cried out in indignation, "The man that hath done this thing shall surely die!" Yet that was the very thing that Nathan wanted to do, to arouse again David's nobler nature. Then, when he was swept by noble emotions, of which he above all men was capable, Nathan drove home his sword, "Thou art the man!"

How could David have missed the point of the parable even for a moment? Only because sin has this strange power to blind us to its presence. Until conscience is awakened, all sin looks odious to our eyes save our own. But now David's conscience is awakened. He sees himself just as Nathan had described that rich man who took the poor man's lamb. With all his possessions and riches and servants and wives, David had robbed the home of that faithful soldier, Uriah, and had taken his wife. There was no resentment against the preacher who exposed his sin, no foolish effort to exculpate himself, as Saul so frequently did when charged with sin. All that he said was "I have sinned." Then David is turned from a man against God's heart to a man after God's heart, for there is nothing in man that God so loves as repentance.

Now, Angels of Heaven, ye who hanged your harps on the branches of the Tree of Life, when ye heard of David's fall, and have not struck a chord or sung a single note since, now, Angels, take down your harps, for once again you can sweep their chords as you sing that sweetest of all songs, the song that tells the joy of heaven over one sinner that repenteth, for David has come back to God! And David himself with his own harp, will sing with you as he forever teaches transgressors the ways of God.

The fifty-first psalm is the inspired record of David's repentance. "Against thee, thee only, have I sinned, and done this evil in thy sight." Men have asked how David could have said that, "Against thee,

thee only, have I sinned." Had he not sinned against Bath-sheba? Had he not sinned against Uriah, the loyal unsuspecting soldier who fell in the forefront of the hottest battle? Had he not sinned against the little child born only to die? Yes, he had sinned against all of them; but David was right when he said that, "Against thee, thee only, have I sinned," because God alone is without sin. He is the One above all others against whom we sin. Can we get that back into Christian faith? Can we get that back into the church, that conviction, that thought of transgression, which was the fountain of so much that was good and strong in our Christian faith, the extreme sinfulness of sin, and how every sin of every kind is a sin against God?

If David warns us against sin, he also shows us how to repent. He illustrates and reveals what are called the "sure mercies of David." Those sure mercies we shall all need. The sincerity of David's repentance is shown by what he said in that great psalm, "Cast me not away from thy presence; and take not thy holy spirit from me." It was not the loss of his kingdom, the loss of his life, the loss of his pleasures, that troubled David, but the fear that he might lose the presence of God. There, indeed, he was the man after God's heart, because, above all else, he treasured the friendship of God.

David did not lose the friendship of God. No

true penitent ever did. At the same time, David was punished. Because of the heinousness of his sin, because of the way in which it would make men scoff and mock and sinners rejoice, even down to this day when they point the finger of scorn at David, Nathan told him that the sword should never depart from his house. And it never did! The sword flashes, and the child, the most innocent in the whole transaction, dies. The sword flashes again, and Amnon deflowers his sister. The sword flashes again, and Absalom buries his dagger in his brother's breast. The sword flashes again, and Absalom's rebellion drives David from his throne. The sword flashes once again, and when the runner out of the Wood of Ephraim in answer to David's question, "Is it well with the young man Absalom?" replied, "The enemies of my Lord the King be as that young man is," David covered his face with his mantle and went up to the chamber over the gate. As he went he said, "O my son, Absalom, my son, my son Absalom! Would God I had died for thee!" No, greatly forgiven though David was, there is nothing in his history which suggests the least alteration in that sentence of God's Word, "Be sure your sins will find you out."

When David wrote his psalm of repentance, he made a singular, yet beautiful request. He told God that if he would only forgive him, and make him to hear joy and gladness again, and create a clean heart within him, and restore unto him the joy of his salvation, then he would teach transgressors God's ways, and sinners should be converted unto him. And God took him at his word. David, greatly, deeply, terribly sinning, was greatly, deeply, beautifully forgiven. And since then, and today, and to the remotest age, till the whole Church of God is saved to sin no more, David will teach transgressors God's ways. He will teach them as he teaches us today, that the greatest possession of life is the friendship of God, and yet that the possession of that friendship makes a man a mark for Satan and his wiles; that all of us must need be on our guard lest we fall into temptation. David tells us that sin is sure to find us out and punish us; but also that God loves to forgive, and that the man who has wandered farthest away from the heart of God may by repentance and faith, and in the infinite mercy of God, be restored unto his favor.

A man after God's heart! Who can tell the wonder and the glory of that? To describe such a man, we would have to tell all that God had in mind when he said at the creation, "Let us make man in our image." That will be the splendor and glory of heaven, and that is the beauty and splendor of Christian life here on earth, a man whose nature has been conformed unto the image of Christ. How wonderful that David, wandering so far and sinning so deeply, could through repentance and faith be restored unto the favor of God, and become again a man after God's own heart! That high and splendid goal is possible for you and me. All that the Triune God could do with David, or Paul, he can do with you. Is that your desire? Is that your ambition? Is that your prayer? To become a man after God's heart? To have your name written forever in the Lamb's Book of Life? If it is, then all the infinite powers of Heaven are with you and for you to bring you to that glorious end!

III

MOSES—THE MAN OF THREE MOUNTAINS

> "My servant Moses .... who is faithful in all mine house."
>
> NUMBERS 12:7

AND SO FAITHFUL THROUGH HIS LONG LIFE, THAT God said he would not speak to Moses in the usual manner of revelation, through dark speeches, but mouth to mouth and face to face.

That is always the way in which the Bible refers to Moses. Always he is the "servant of the Lord," the man who does God's will. We can follow Moses further than almost any character of the Bible. We know his story from the river cradle to that solitary grave where God buried him on Nebo's lonely mountain; and wherever we see him or hear him through those 120 years of his life, he is the "servant of the Lord."

The three most influential men of the Bible, influential because of the importance and result of what they established and did in their day and generation, are Abraham, Moses and Paul. These are the three towering mountain peaks of biblical biography. The Jews were not content with the sublime record in the Book of Deuteronomy which tells us of the death of Moses on Pisgah and Nebo. They felt that Moses was so great in soul and intellect, and the work that he had accomplished so inestimable in importance, that they tried to add something to the splendor of that solitary entombment on Mount Nebo.

According to the old legend, God commanded the supreme angels to take away the soul of Moses. The first of these was the angel Zangiel who had been the instructor and teacher of Moses. But this angel pleaded to be released from that commission because Moses had been his disciple. Then the Angel of Death was called forth, and always eager for his melancholy triumph, drew his sword and approached Moses. But when he saw the Ineffable Name inscribed on the rod of Moses, and the wonderful lustre on his countenance, he turned away in fear. As he did so, a voice sounded from heaven speaking to Moses, "Contend not; thy life lasteth only a short moment."

A second time the Angel of Death was commanded to take away the soul of Moses, and once again he went forth with drawn sword. But when he lifted his sword to smite Moses, Moses touched him with his staff, upon which was inscribed the Divine Name. And with that the Angel of Death fled the second time.

But again the voice sounded from heaven, speaking to Moses, "The end of thy time hath come." Moses then made this prayer to God: "Thou Lord of the Universe, who wast revealed to me in the burning bush, remember that thou didst carry me up into thy heaven, where I abode forty days and forty nights. Have mercy upon me and hand me not over into the power of the Angel of Death."

The prayer of Moses was granted, and the Almighty removed the soul of Moses with a kiss. Such is the interpretation that legend gives to the verse from Deuteronomy, "So Moses the servant of the Lord died there in the land of Moab according to the word of the Lord." When Moses died there was sorrow on earth and sorrow in heaven at the passing of so great a servant of the Lord.

How strange was the beginning of that great life. In Egypt a Levite and his wife gave birth to a little child. By the monstrous edict of Pharaoh the parents themselves were bound to destroy their own child by casting him into the river Nile. Spies watched the birth chambers of the Jews to see that this cruel command was obeyed and that no male child was permitted to live. But this father and mother saw that their child was "a goodly child." All fathers and mothers, I suppose, when they look upon their child at birth, see that he is a goodly child. That was what the parents of Moses saw when he was born. When a child is born into a home he is ever a goodly child, and the light of goodly hopes crowns his brow. All the struggle, travail, anguish, heartbreak, disappointment, sickness, disease, tragedy, and transgression of mankind are forgotten when a new child comes into the world. It is in a very real sense a new creation, and those who have brought the child into the world, do all they can to hide him, and hide themselves, from the world's labor and sorrow.

When they saw that he was a goodly child they hid Moses for three months around the house, and when it was impossible longer to secrete him, his mother made a little cradle for him out of bulrushes and daubed it with slime and pitch. Only a cradle of bulrushes, and daubed with slime and pitch, and yet never did loving maternal hands put more of a mother's soul and a mother's heart into the making of a cradle and the garments for its little occupant. By night they carried the babe and his cradle down to the river Nile. Never was a child more tenderly laid in his cradle than Moses that night by the hand of his faithful mother. When the rising sun made it dangerous for her to linger longer, she gave her babe a last kiss, took a last look at him, and then went back to the city, leaving Miriam, the sister, to watch and see what might happen.

When the morning came there was the Nile, flowing broadly away as it has done through the ages. And yonder along the banks of the Nile on the earthen dykes passed the procession of animals and peasants going forth to their labor. Over the river towered the great sails of the Nile boats, higher than the stately palms which line the banks of the stream; and far in the distance loomed the great pyramids.

How much of the world's hope was vested in that frail cradle rocking there in the waters of the Nile, with the infant looking up at the lotus flowers which bent over it. Only that ark of bulrushes was between the child and the river, and only the lotus flowers along the banks screened him from the murderous hand of Pharaoh. Yet the child was safe because he represented the great purpose and plan of God.

As Miriam waited she heard the sound of footsteps. Presently, black Numidian slaves passed by, carrying on their shoulders a richly adorned palanquin, in which sat the beautiful princess of Egypt. She has come down to the river to bathe, not on the other side of the river, and not further up the bank of the river, where the trees and the vegetation would have hidden the cradle of Moses, but on this side of the river, and at the very place where the child lay gazing at the blue Egyptian sky. When she saw the child the maternal instincts of the princess were aroused. God planned to save Moses in order that he might deliver his people out of Egypt. But see how he did it. First of all, there was the love of that father and mother, and then the affection and pity of the princess of Egypt, Pharaoh's daughter. Truly God works in a mysterious way his wonders to perform. Moses, who is to be the incarnation of God's plan, is saved from death and destruction by the very river that was to have destroyed him and by the very daughter of the ruler who had issued the monstrous decree for his death.

Time would fail to tell here of the great choice that Moses made when he slew the Egyptian whom he saw wronging a Hebrew and thus refused to be called the son of Pharoah's daughter, casting in his lot with the people of God and fleeing into the land of Midian. Moses saw an Egyptian smiting a Hebrew. That, alas, has been the history of the Hebrew from generation to generation. Whenever you see him, somebody is smiting him, Egyptian, Midianite, Canaanite, Assyrian, Babylonian, Roman, Russian, Spaniard, and now German. Yet the Jew has not perished. The hammer that has smitten him has always been broken. So far as God's word is concerned, that is the chief assurance concerning the present world situation. The nation that has so cruelly, wickedly, and so bloodily smitten the Jew cannot in the end conquer, else all the mighty voices of history speak to us in vain.

MOSES—MAN OF THREE MOUNTAINS

Time would fail to tell, too, of the call of Moses. It seemed that he was doomed to the inconspicuous life of a shepherd buried in the wilds of Midian. But when the bush burned, and Moses turned aside to see and to hear, God told him that on that very mountain which now rose above the plains he and the delivered people of Israel would come to worship God.

I

THE MOUNTAIN OF REVELATION

Moses I call the Man of Three Mountains. The first of these mountains is the Mountain of Revelation.

God called Moses up into the mount, and there, when the mountain smoked and the earth quaked, and there were lightnings and thunders, the words of the Law, the Ten Commandments, were given to Moses. "The law came by Moses," John said. Not *from* Moses, but *by* Moses. Moses was the one chosen of God to receive that great revelation which was to be the foundation of the structure of the civilization of future ages, the foundation of the Church of the Living God, the source whence flows the stream of morality.

The world seems to be at the parting of the ways today. More and more men and nations divide into two groups. On the one side are those who recognize no authority, no guidance, no control, no inspiration save that of their own desires and their own purposes and ambitions. Man himself is the law unto himself. On the other side are those who, however they may fail to live up to it, recognize a higher law and a higher order than man himself. Today we have nations, armed to the teeth, which frankly disavow any regard for the authority of the Ten Commandments or for the religion which has spread them throughout the world. The only law is the law of force and the will of man. On the other side are nations which, with all their faults, still recognize that there are spiritual and moral laws which come from a higher power and which are supreme.

Which way is the world going to turn? Will it turn more and more to this worship of man and to the law of force? Or will it turn back to the law of God? Were one to judge by surface and contemporary events, one would almost conclude that everything that is represented by the Ten Commandments and a revealed religion, the authority of God, and the authority of Christ, belief in the soul and the immortality of the soul, will be submerged, and every star in the heavens of mankind will be darkened. On the other hand is the long survival from age to age of spiritual and moral truth. The

Kingdom of God has never been shaken down, either as a hope or as a fact. Again and again, when the convulsions were over and the angry waters had subsided, the sacred heights of Sinai and Calvary again appeared above the abyss, and mankind again bowed in reverence to those truths which God gave to Moses on the mount and which were fulfilled in the life and teaching of Him who died upon the Cross.

II

THE MOUNTAIN OF INTERCESSION

The second mountain is the Mountain of Intercession.

Moses was a mighty interceder—as the greatest of souls have ever been. The first Mount of Intercession was at Rephidim. The people had been delivered out of Egypt, had crossed the Red Sea and had come as far is Rephidim, where they were assailed by the fierce tribesmen who inherited the land, the Amalekites. This was a critical day in the history of Israel. The people had not yet met a foe in battle. Moses directed Joshua to lead the battle against the Amalekites on the plains below, while he and Aaron and Hur went to the top of the mountain that overlooked the plain. There Moses lifted up his rod toward heaven. This was the rod which was a symbol of God's presence and power. It was the rod which he had stretched over the Nile, and it was turned to blood; the rod which he had stretched towards heaven, and thick darkness came down over Egypt; the rod with which he had smitten the rock and water gushed forth to quench the people's thirst; the rod which he had stretched out over the waters of the Red Sea, and they fell back and left a pathway for the people of Israel.

As long as Moses held aloft the rod, in that act of faith and of prayer, the children of Israel prevailed in the battle below; but Moses was an aged man, and even for the most robust it would have been an impossible task to hold the rod on high, hour after hour. When Moses grew weary and the rod came down, then the Amalekites prevailed. Seeing this, Aaron and Hur set Moses on a great stone, and standing one on one side and one on the other, they held up his hands all through that critical day until the victory was won.

So it has always been. Where the church does its work in prayer and in faith, it will in some real way prevail over the Amalekites that everywhere assail it in this present world. Where it forgets to pray, and the stars of great faith go out, then the church becomes just another society, another organization in the world. This is true also of the soul, of your soul and my soul. When you stop praying, when you get away from God, when you get away from his word, then Amalek, the power of this present world, the power of evil, will prevail in your life.

Moses made another great prayer when he came down from the mount and found that the people had built a golden calf and were worshiping it. The rage and disgust of Moses, manifested by the way in which he took the two tables of stone and crashed them in fragments on the ground, were followed by that deep and moving intercession for the guilty and idolatrous people. God had said that he would destroy the people because of their great sin, for the people had corrupted themselves. But Moses pled with God to spare them once more. So earnest and eager was his prayer that he said, "Yet now, if thou wilt forgive their sin—; and if not, blot me, I pray thee, out of thy book which thou hast written." For the sake of his people Moses is willing to be blotted out of the Book of Life. And great Paul, too, said the same thing, that he could wish himself accursed, even blotted out of the Book of Life, if only God would save Israel. These great souls have the burden of other souls upon them. Is not that our great lack today—that ministers, people, churches, do not feel the burden of souls that Abraham felt when he pleaded with God for Sodom and Gomorrah, that Moses felt when he pleaded with God to spare the people, that Christ felt when he looked upon the multitude as sheep without a shepherd and was moved with compassion? Moses had a great heart. That is what made him a great man.

III

THE MOUNTAIN OF DISAPPOINTMENT

Now we come to the third mountain, the Mountain of Disappointment, or Mount Pisgah and Nebo.

The great work had been accomplished. Moses had led the people out of Egypt and through the forty years of wandering in the wilderness. Now he had brought them to the borders of the Promised Land. Over there was the great goal which had inspired him through all his labors. But Moses was not to enter the Land of Promise. For what to us, with our own sinful hearts, seems a trivial offense, that when God told him to speak to the rock and bring forth water for the people, in his anger and impatience at their murmuring and rebellion, Moses smote the rock *twice,* and cried, "Hear now, ye rebels; must we fetch you water out of the rock" —because of this transgression, because he had not sanctified God in the eyes of the people, Moses was told that he could not enter the Promised Land.

God told him to climb to the top of Pisgah, or Nebo, where he would die and be gathered unto his people. When Aaron died and was stripped of his priestly vestments, Moses and Eleazer went with him; but all alone Moses ascended the mountain which was to be his sepulcher. From Pisgah's top Moses could see spread out before him the great panorama of the Promised Land. At the foot of the mountain lay the Twelve Tribes of Israel, with the Ark in their midst and the standards waving in the morning breeze. Just across the Jordan was Jericho, the City of the Palm Trees. To the north were the hills and mountains that overlooked the lovely Sea of Galilee, and far in the distance towering above all other mountains, Hermon's snow-covered peak. On the hills beyond Jordan lay the site of the Jerusalem that was to be, and yonder was Bethlehem, where Moses' great successor was to be born. And far beyond all flashed the waves of the Great Sea itself. Moses drank it in like an inhalation. There was the goal, there was the land to which he had led the people; but it was not for him. God said to him, "I have caused thee to see it with thine eyes, but thou shalt not go over thither." "So Moses the servant of the Lord died there in the land of Moab, according to the word of the Lord."

That will ever be true, I suppose, of the highest desires that come to us and the visions that break upon our view in this life. We see them, we salute them, we rejoice in them; but not here, not on this side of the river of Death, not in this life, do we possess them. "Thou shalt see it with thine eyes." The deepest satisfactions and the true fulfillments are in the life to come. Here we have no abiding city, but there are the eternal habitations.

Moses was not permitted to cross over into the Promised Land. But now the ages have passed, and the great Prophet to whom Moses looked forward and of whom he wrote, has come. On the Mount of Transfiguration Christ is transfigured in glory; and two men, Moses and Elijah, appear in glory and speak of his decease which he should accomplish at Jerusalem. Centuries before that day, it looked like a disappointment, almost an injustice, for Moses only to see that land with his eyes, and not be permitted to enter. But now God's ways are plain. Moses stands on the mount in the Promised Land, by the side of the Son of God, and with mighty Elijah, talks with him about the work of atonement which he is to carry out upon the cross.

Thus the disappointment of Moses speaks to our souls. Yonder on Nebo's lonely mountain, on this side Jordan's strand, we learn that God has his own mysteries of grace, ways that now we cannot understand, and which he hides deep like the hidden sleep of him he loved so well. Give God time! Wait, I say, on the Lord! Forbidden to enter the Promised Land, Moses with the whole company of God's redeemed now stands by the Sea of Glass mingled with Fire and sings the "Song of Moses, the servant of God, and the song of the Lamb, saying, Great and marvelous are thy works, Lord God Almighty; just and true are thy ways, thou king of saints." Yes, that will be the great harmony, that the grandest of all songs, when all our labors and wanderings and trials and temptations and disappointments and battles ended, redeemed by the Blood of the Lamb, we shall stand upon that Sea of Glass mingled with Fire and sing the Song of Moses and the Lamb.

IV

JOHN—THAT DISCIPLE WHOM JESUS LOVED

"That disciple whom Jesus loved."
JOHN 21:7

A FRIEND OF SIR PHILIP SIDNEY, WHO DIED ON THE field of Zutphen after uttering his famous sentence, "Thy need is greater than mine," desired that the following epitaph be placed on his grave:

"Here lies Sir Philip Sidney's friend."

John, too, chose and wrote his own epitaph, and here it is—than which a greater has never been written—"That disciple whom Jesus loved."

There are times when I am certain that Paul is the greatest character in Christian history. When I think of his dramatic conversion at Damascus, and how the chief enemy of Christ became his greatest friend; when I think of his extraordinary sacrifices and hardships and sufferings by land and by sea; when I think of the remarkable combination of intellect and emotion and organizing ability; when I remember his grand statements of Christian truth and life, and how the greater part of the New Testament came from his pen, I feel certain that Paul is the greatest Christian personality.

At other times I wonder if Peter is not the greatest Christian. When I remember how Christ told him, when he called him, that his name would be Peter, "The Rock"; when I recall how Christ spoke to him more often than to any other apostle, how Christ answered his numerous questions, how he praised him, rebuked him, prayed over him, warned him, gave him a special resurrection message and appearance, and when he restored him gave him a special commission to "Feed my sheep"; and when I see the place that Peter takes in the establishment of the Christian church, I conclude that Peter must be the greatest Christian personality.

But I have other moods when I conclude that John is the greatest Christian character. When I read those deep, opening sentences of his Gospel, "In the beginning was the Word, and the Word was with God, and the Word was God"; when I quote by the side of the dying and the sorrowing the beautiful words of John's Gospel, "Let not your heart be troubled: ye believe in God, believe also in me"; when I hear him describe himself as "that disciple whom Jesus loved"; when I hear him say that "God is Love," and that "everyone that loveth is born of God and knoweth God"; and when I behold the horizon of the world's sky aglow with the light and splendor of the Holy City of God, the New Jerusalem; and when I hear the mighty roll of the thunder of the Apocalypse, or listen to the murmur of the River of Water of Life, I conclude that John is the greatest Christian personality.

But each one—Paul, Peter, and John—has his own place. Each is altogether different from the other two. The church could never have done without Paul; it could never have done without Peter, and it could never have done without John. David had his "Three Mighty Men," beyond all others in valor and distinction. Likewise, the Son of David had his three mighty men, and these are, Paul, Peter, and John.

In a memorable interview with Peter and John after his resurrection, Jesus, foretelling the death by which Peter was to glorify God, said to him, "When thou shalt be old, thou shalt stretch forth thy hands, and another shall gird thee, and carry thee whither thou wouldest not." Then Peter asked one of his characteristic, impulsive questions. Seeing John standing near, Peter said to Jesus, "And what shall this man do?" Jesus answered him, "If I will that he tarry till I come, what is that to thee? Follow thou me." Because of that saying of Christ, the idea got abroad among the early Christians that John was not going to die. John himself dismisses that misunderstanding by reminding the readers of his Gospel that Jesus did not say he was not to die, but, *"If I will* that he tarry till I come, what is that to thee?"

What did that mean, "If I will that he tarry till I come"? Some have taken it to mean that the coming to which Jesus refers is his coming in judgment at the destruction of Jerusalem, and that John was to live until the destruction of Jerusalem. As a historic fact it is fairly well established that John did live until the destruction of Jerusalem. In harmony with this is the fact that of the four Gospels, John's is the only one in which there is no prophecy of the destruction of Jerusalem—an altogether natural thing if John wrote his Gospel after the destruction of Jerusalem. Others again have taken the words of Christ to be a mere supposition on his part. He does not say that John is to live until he comes, but, "Suppose he should live? What then? Suppose that is the plan for John's life? What is that to thee? You have your duty and responsibility, and that is to follow me."

Others again have given a somewhat figurative interpretation of the words of Jesus, making them mean that until Christ shall come again the apostle John, through his Gospel, his three Letters, and the Book of Revelation will be the chief witness to the Lord Jesus Christ and his kingdom. I am not sure that we shall put the witness of John in his person and in his writings above that of Paul. But until Christ comes, there is no doubt that John through his person, his Gospel, his Letters, and the Apocalypse will be a chief witness to Christ and his kingdom.

I

JOHN'S DECISION

All the disciples were called of Christ and made their decision to follow him. John himself, although he hides his own name, gives us the beautiful story of his first meeting with Christ. It was by the River Jordan, the second day after the Baptism of Jesus by John the Baptist. Andrew and the "other disciple," who must have been John, were in the company of John the Baptist when Jesus passed by. When they heard John exclaim, "Behold, the Lamb of God!" they turned and followed Jesus; and Jesus, knowing that they were following him, turned about and said, "What seek ye?" They, probably a little taken aback, and not knowing just what to answer, replied, "Master, where dwellest thou?" He said unto them, "Come and see." Andrew and John followed Jesus to the place where he was living. That was John's introduction to Christ. Apparently, just a chance meeting, and yet what if they had never met! What if Jesus had never passed by! What if Jesus had never said to them, "Come and see"!

How much poorer our Bible would be today, how much dimmer our hope for the future, and how much less music there would be in heaven tonight! But John saw him and heard him, and went with him and became his disciple. It must have been fifty years afterward, when John, now no longer the youngest of the disciples, but John the aged, and probably the sole survivor of the disciples, wrote his Gospel. But that meeting with Christ was just as fresh then as it was on the evening of that memorable day, for John remembers not only the day but the hour of the day, just how high the sun was over the Syrian hills, for he says, "It was about the tenth hour." That will always be your greatest hour—the hour when first you knew the Lord.

II

JOHN'S ENTHUSIASM AND COURAGE

In Leonardo's great painting of Jesus and the Disciples at the Last Supper, I have always felt that his John is a failure. There is nothing in the gospel records which would lead us to believe that John was the mild, effeminate character portrayed by the brush of Leonardo. There is nothing there to suggest the eagle, John's symbol in church history, or the Son of Thunder, as he was known, with his brother James.

John was a man of fiery zeal and enthusiasm; so much so, that on two occasions Jesus had to rebuke him—once, when John had rebuked a man not of the disciple's band who was casting out devils in the name of Christ, and again, when John wanted to call down fire on a Samaritan village, immortal for its incivility to Jesus. John's zeal overflowed somewhat on the side of intolerance; but Jesus would rather have a disciple like that than one who has no convictions. We hear a great deal today about intolerance. It is the stale and platitudinous theme of many public speakers and writers; but so far as Christianity is concerned, the great danger is not intolerance, but the lack of any conviction whatsoever, and an indifference which tolerates every kind of belief and unbelief and every kind of conduct.

John, with James, wanted a seat at Christ's right hand when the Master came to establish his throne. That is far more than most Christians desire. Christ did not rebuke John on that occasion, but only reminded him of the price of such a seat. "Are ye able to drink my cup?" And John, with James, said he was ready to drink the cup.

John was a courageous man, too. He went like a lion into the Court of the High Priest. Apparently, he was the only apostle who had the courage to be present at the Crucifixion of Jesus. He was put to the ultimate test by the Roman authorities, and, probably under the reign of Domitian, because of his loyalty to Jesus was sentenced to cruel imprisonment on the Isle of Patmos. That is what he means in the prologue to the Book of Revelation, where he says, "I John, who also am your brother, and companion in tribulation, and in the kingdom and patience of Jesus Christ, was in the isle that is called Patmos for the Word of God, and for the testimony of Jesus Christ." John is a man who teaches you and inspires you to have the courage to stand for your faith and witness to Christ.

III

JOHN, THE MAN OF TENDERNESS

This man of conviction and courage and flaming zeal, this Son of Thunder, was also a son of consolation. John is the man of tenderness. Beware of the man who has no vein of tenderness in him, and especially beware of the woman who has no vein of tenderness in her. There are several instances of John's tenderness related in the Gospels. One is how he took Peter after a shameful denial of his Lord into his own house. John did not cast Peter out because he had fallen and denied his Lord, but he took him into his own home, and in those black, terrible hours must have comforted him and consoled him. Then there was that great scene at the Cross when Jesus commended Mary His Mother to the care of John. This is the way John puts it: "When Jesus therefore saw his mother, and the disciple standing by whom he loved, he saith unto his mother, Woman, behold thy son! Then saith he to the disciple, Behold thy mother! And from that hour that disciple took her unto his own home." Yes, among all the disciples, John was the one into whose keeping Jesus committed his mother.

But there was another and very moving instance of John's tenderness. This is how he describes himself at the Last Supper. "Now there was leaning on Jesus' bosom one of his disciples, whom Jesus loved." That sentence itself is sufficient to prove the inspiration of the Bible. Who but an inspired man could have written it? Uriel, Angel of the Light, standing in the sun, tell me, couldst thou have written it? Raphael, Angel of Reason, tell me, couldst thou have written that sentence? Michael, Angel of the Sword, couldst thou have written it? Gabriel, Angel of Prophetic Song, couldst thou have written that sentence? No! Only John could have written it, only John who was leaning on Jesus' bosom at the Supper.

The disciples that night were quarrelling over the first places, the places of honor in Christ's kingdom; but John did not dispute or quarrel. He had the place he wanted, the bosom of Jesus. Philip asked Jesus difficult questions that night, "Shew us the

Father, and it sufficeth us." But not so John. He knew that he that hath seen the Son hath seen the Father. Always melancholy Thomas said in his despondent mood to Jesus, "We know not whither thou goest; and how can we know the way?" But John did not ask about the way, for he had reached the end of the way, the breast of Christ. He was leaning on Jesus' bosom.

Judas, not Iscariot, asked Jesus that night, "Lord, how is it that thou wilt manifest thyself unto us, and not unto the world?" But John did not ask that question, for he knew already the answer that Jesus gave, "If a man love me, he will keep my words: and my Father will love him, and we will come unto him, and make our abode with him." John knew that already, as he leaned on Jesus' bosom at the Supper.

Peter was loudly boasting that night that though all should forsake Jesus and flee, he would not; and yet before the cock crew he had denied his Lord thrice. But John had no need to boast, and no need to fear. John was the tranquil one that night. Leaning on the bosom of Jesus, he knew that he was safe; he knew that he could not deny or forsake Jesus.

Judas Iscariot was soon to go out into the night and betray his Lord for thirty pieces of silver, but John could not have done that, for already he had the wealth that his soul desired—he was leaning on

Jesus' bosom. No, John did not doubt or despair. John did not deny or betray that night, for he was leaning on Jesus' bosom. That ever will be the place of safety for the disciples of Christ. John, move over, and make room for me!

IV

JOHN, THE PROPHETIC MAN

At four o'clock on a summer morning I went on deck. Noiselessly the ship was gliding into a landlocked harbor; and then with the rattling of anchor chains it came to a standstill. In front of me I saw a dark mass rising out of the sea. In the heavens above the brilliant stars were still shining. A small boat put off from the steamer and we were rowed to the landing place. Now the stars were beginning to pale and the sun rising in the east was beginning to gild the placid sea, and touch with gold the tops of the mountains. Absolute silence. Silence on the sea. Silence on the land. Deep silence, like that which was in heaven for half an hour when John saw and heard the wonders of the Apocalypse. This was the isle which was called Patmos. This was the isle of John's vision, where he saw the sea of glass mingled with fire and heard the triumphant song of the ten thousand times ten thousand.

This Book of John is the book of the hour. Are

we told, what seems to be true, that the spiritual and moral lamps of the world are burning lower and dimmer than for many a day? Are we told that the spiritual riches accumulated through the ages by mankind are likely to be destroyed? Do we stand in dread at the fearful outbreak of satanic violence and unbelief and at all the rage of Antichrist in the world? If so, read the Apocalypse! All that the tyrants and despots and dictators do, or threaten to do, is there in John's wonderful book. There all the rage of the Beast out of the abyss is described and foretold; all that Satan plans against the Church of Christ, every mask and disguise which he wears, every war that he makes upon the saints, every apostasy of the Church, every long night of waiting and watching, and at length, the final and glorious triumph when he who on the cross cried, "It is finished," shall from the throne of a regenerated universe, cry, "It is done," and when the kingdoms of this world shall have become the kingdoms of our Lord—all that is declared here in John's great book. Read John's book, and lift up your hearts and rejoice.

Now, in closing, let me tell you a very remarkable thing about that Last Supper. Jesus had said that one of his disciples that night would betray him, and now Peter, the man who was always asking questions, at the right time or the wrong time, impetuous, impulsive Peter, instead of asking Jesus himself, this time asked John to ask the question for him. Peter beckoned to John who was leaning on Jesus' bosom, and said, "John, you ask him."

Yes, that will ever be true. When it comes to the great things of the soul, to the great things of the Christian life, ask John to ask Jesus about it. When the bitter cup of sorrow and grief is pressed to your lips, ask John to ask Jesus, and John will tell you the answer of Jesus, "Let not your heart be troubled: ye believe in God, believe also in me." When you want a lamp or a lantern by which to light your path in the night and which the winds of time cannot blow out, ask John to ask Jesus and he will give you that lantern, "Little children, love one another." When your sins threaten you and overwhelm you, ask John to ask Jesus about them, and he will tell you, "The blood of Jesus Christ his Son cleanseth us from all sin." When aghast at the rage of Satan and Antichrist in the world about you, you wonder what will be the issue of the long struggle between good and evil, light and darkness, Satan and Christ, ask John to ask Jesus, and he will tell you, "I John saw the holy city, new Jerusalem, coming down from God out of heaven."

V

PETER—THE MAN WHO WAS SAVED BY A LOOK

> "And Peter went out, and wept bitterly."
> LUKE 22:62

IN MY DREAM I CAME TO THE CELESTIAL CITY, where all was glorious and fair. My soul was ravished with the beauty that I saw and the music that I heard, harpers harping with their harps, and the ten thousand times ten thousand praising the Lamb that was slain. At first, however, I knew not just where to go or with what company to associate myself, for in that Shining City I saw many throngs assembled. One of the archangels, seeing my hesitation and perplexity, came forward and accosted me. He asked me if I would like him to conduct me to one of the assemblies that I saw. I told him that I was not sure which one to choose; but pointing to a company gathered together under the Tree of Life on the banks of the River of Life, I asked him who these might be. "These," he replied, "are they who are gathered about Paul, and if you join them now, you will hear his high discourse on the sovereignty of God, predestination, and redeeming grace." I told the archangel that Paul had been my first love and greatest study among all the apostles and the heroes of the Faith. Greatly did I desire to see him and to hear him; and yet perhaps I would not feel altogether at home in that august company gathered about the apostle, for Paul was so mighty, so preeminent, so heroic in his Christian race, so altogether in his Christian life without a fault or flaw. "I am not sure," I said, "that I would feel at home there."

Then, beholding another company standing by the Sea of Glass mingled with Fire, I asked the archangel who these might be. "These," he answered, "are the friends of John, and although they are now in heaven and drink of the Water of Life at its source, still they delight to hear mystic John discourse on the nature of God and how God is Love. If you join them now, you will hear John speak on the transformation of redeemed men into the likeness of the image of God." When I heard this, I started eagerly in the direction of that company standing by the Sea of Glass; but after a few steps I came to a pause. The archangel, seeing me stop and hesitate, joined me again and said, "Why do you hesitate? Would you not like to join this company who listen to the rapt and mystic speech of John?" For answer I said, "Ardently have I wished to see and hear that disciple who leaned upon the breast of Jesus at the Supper, and who saw a door opened for him into heaven; and yet, perhaps, John attracts to his company only those who have lived in the highest sense in loyalty to his beautiful command of love for God and love for man, and who have not felt as other souls have felt the darkening clouds of sin. Perhaps I had better seek some other company, for I might feel a little ill at ease in the company now gathered about John."

"Then," said my heavenly guide, "perhaps you would like to join yonder throng, for it is by far the most numerous of all the companies of heaven," pointing as he said this toward the western wall of the city, on the foundations of which I could make out the names of the Twelve Apostles of the Lamb. Looking in that direction, I saw a great company which no man could number. "Whose company is that?" I said to the angel. "That," he said, "is the company of those who listen to the voice of Peter." When he said that, my heart leaped within me, for I was sure that I would feel at home in the company of those assembled about Peter. I was certain they would be in many respects like him—weak, impulsive, sometimes cowardly, sometimes unfaithful, but penitent and redeemed men. Yes, that was the place for me! Eagerly I hastened forward to join that immense throng. When I reached the outskirts of that great company I could hear the loud, ringing voice of Peter, much as I had expected it would sound, because of what I had read of him in the Gospels and in the Acts of the Apostles.

And what, think you, was the theme of Peter's discourse, listened to with such eager, rapt attention by this great multitude which no man could number? What was the theme that drew such a response as I saw written on these faces, faces that had known sin and sorrow and failure, and the bitterness of grief, faces that were illuminated, too, with the light of repentance and forgiveness, and the joy of the Lord? Was it the story of that scene in the desert place at Caesarea Philippi, when Peter confessed that Jesus was the Christ the Son of God, and Christ said that upon that truth he would build his church, and the gates of hell could not prevail against it? Was it the story of that stormy night on Galilee when Peter tried to walk on the sea? Was it the story of the night on the mountain when Jesus was transfigured before them and they saw Moses and Elijah talking with him? Was it the story of that wonderful morning by the Sea of Galilee when they saw Jesus on the shore, and Peter leaped into the sea and swam to where he was, and heard his threefold question, "Lovest thou me?" Was it the story of the Day of the Ascension on Olivet's Mount when the cloud received him out of their sight? Was it the story of the Day of Pentecost when fire fell from heaven and Peter preached his great sermon and brought five thousand souls into the kingdom? Was it the story of that beautiful incident at the Gate Beautiful of the Temple when Peter and John healed the lame man? Was it the story of that wonderful night in Herod's prison, when at midnight, while the church in Mary's house was praying for him, and Peter lay bound between the soldiers, an angel smote him on the side, and he arose and followed the angel and passed through the first and second wards and came unto the iron gate, which opened unto him of its own accord?

No! It was not of these great hours and great scenes that I heard Peter now discoursing to that multitude by the city's western wall. It was the story of that night when he denied his Lord.

Last Sunday night I asked the angels—Uriel the Angel of Light; Raphael, the Angel of Reason; Michael, the Angel of the Sword; and Gabriel, the Angel of Holy Song—if any of them could have written that verse about John, "Now there was leaning on Jesus' bosom that disciple whom Jesus loved." Tonight I would like to ask these angels another question. Tell me, angels and archangels, ye who gaze upon the great White Throne itself, could any of you have written this verse about Peter, "And Peter went out, and wept bitterly"? Tell me, could any of you have related this story that is told in all the four Gospels, the story how Peter cursed and denied his Lord, and how his Lord looked upon him and Peter went out into the night and wept bitterly?

We can learn more from Peter than from all other of the Twelve Disciples put together. His impulsive deeds, his frequent questions, his eager exclamations and confessions, the praise and honor and rebukes that were bestowed upon him, his sometimes manly and sometimes cowardly acts, his oaths, his bitter tears—all this makes Peter the great companion and the great instructor of his fellow men and his fellow Christians. In a sense, he is an epitome of Christianity. Much as we can learn from Peter on all these occasions, we learn more from him on this night when he denied his Lord than in all the rest of his life.

I

PETER'S TEMPTATION AND FALL

At the Last Supper, Peter was all that you would like him to be. He was no braggart and idle boaster, but earnest, reverent, affectionate, devoted and courageous. Peter was no common impostor or counterfeit. He was altogether sincere when he said that come what might he would stand by Jesus to the last, and was ready to go with him to prison and to death. Like all of us, Peter was strong when he could not see the temptation, but weak when it appeared.

PETER—WHO WAS SAVED BY A LOOK

On this last night, as on most of the great occasions of his life, it was to Peter that our Lord chiefly addressed himself. After he had spoken of the kingdom that his Father had appointed unto them, he turned to Peter and said, "Simon, behold, Satan hath desired to have you, that he may sift you as wheat: but I have prayed for thee, that thy faith fail not: and when thou art converted, strengthen thy brethren." There we have Peter's temptation, his fall, his repentance, his restoration and his future ministry, all remarkably foretold.

Although he spoke specifically to Peter, what he said about Satan desiring to have him was true of all the disciples. It is true of you and me. The soul of every man, the most valuable thing in all the universe, is the ambition of Christ and the desire of Satan. However little you care for your soul, remember how much Christ cares for it and how much Satan desires to have it.

In the Garden of Gethsemane Peter was no worse than the others who fell asleep while Jesus entered into his agony. Yet it is worth noting that two of the evangelists, Matthew and Mark, whose Gospel was probably the first, and which is often spoken of as Peter's Gospel, relate how it was to Peter that Jesus spoke in amazement when he came and found them sleeping. "Simon, sleepest thou? couldst thou not watch one hour?" As if to say, "I thought,

Simon, that you were the one who was going to be faithful even unto death, and now thou sleepest!" "Sleepest thou?" Does that *"thou"* strike you and me?

When Peter had said that he would never desert his Lord, he was thinking, no doubt, of an attack upon him by His enemies, and he made good his pledge, for when he saw the crowd roughly handling his Master, he drew his sword and aimed a mighty blow at the head of the servant of the high priest. Peter must have been greatly perplexed by the sequel, the rebuke that Christ gave him, when he might have expected praise, and then the submission of Jesus to his captors.

In perplexity and uncertainty, wondering what was going to happen to Christ and his claims, Peter followed that night "afar off," as they led Jesus, bound, from the Garden of Gethsemane to the palace of the high priest. You can see the flickering torches of the mob and hear the coarse murmur of their voices as they lead Jesus away; and away yonder in the background, anxious, unhappy, and yet with love still burning in his heart, Peter follows "afar off."

There, again, Peter comes close to you and me. We would not put ourselves out of the company of Christ altogether. We would not join the ranks of his enemies; and yet is it not often true that the best we do is to follow him "afar off"?

PETER—WHO WAS SAVED BY A LOOK

Peter, Matthew tells us, had come "to see the end," and it was with that in his mind that he took his place with the servants and other loiterers and the foes of Jesus about the fire in the courtyard of the high priest. Whether the end was to be the crucifixion of Jesus or his liberation and enthronement, Peter did not know; but he was determined "to see the end."

The probable order of events in the temptation of Peter was as follows: First, the maid that kept the door said to Peter as she looked into his face by the light of the fire, "Art not thou also one of this man's disciples?" Whereupon, Peter bluntly answered, "I am not." Then, after a little, one of the men who stood by said to him, "Thou also art one of them." Peter answered, "Man, I am not!" Then, after a little, the same maid Peter heard saying to some of them that stood near, "He is one of them," and again denied. Then another man, a relative of the high priest's servant, whose ear Peter had cut off in the garden, said to him, "Did not I see thee in the garden with him?" and Peter again denied his Lord. Then after a while another man said, "You were one of them, for you are a Galilean. I can tell it by your speech." And now Peter not only denied that he was a disciple of Jesus, but began to curse and to swear, and said, "I know not the man!"

If Peter had seen anyone strike Jesus or rush at

him, there is no doubt that he would have lifted his arm or drawn his sword to defend him. But just to sit there by the fire and wait, that was a different thing. He could have attacked the mob, but he went down before a woman's sneer. Mark's Gospel is Peter's Gospel. The other accounts spare Peter as much as possible, and it is only Mark's Gospel—and Luke's which follows Mark—with Peter speaking in it that adds this element of baseness and horror, that when Peter denied his Lord he cursed and swore.

But here again Peter is no monster, no prodigy of iniquity, but a man of like passions with us. Today we can say, "Though all should forsake thee, yet will not I." Today we can sing, "I Am Thine, O Lord." But tomorrow we deny the Christ within us and say, "I never knew you." Was that the only palace hall that has heard the echo of those words? Were Peter's lips the only lips that ever said that, "I never knew you"? And what about that word that the servant of the high priest said to Peter, "Did not I see thee in the garden with him?" And now you sit with his foes and enemies! What about those words? We shall ask that relative of the high priest's servant to repeat them in our hearing. "Minister, did not I see thee in the pulpit with him?" "Singer, did not I see thee in the choir loft with him, singing his praise?" "Elder and church officer, did not I see thee in a meeting of the session with him?" "Sabbath school teacher, did not I see thee in the Sunday school class with him, telling the story of his life?" And now you say to me, "I never knew him"!

II

PETER'S CONVICTION

There were two elements in Peter's conviction. The first was a simple, common, ordinary happening in the natural world. The cock crows. Although Immanuel, the Son of God, is suffering, mocked and beaten, betrayed and denied, the great processes of nature go on. The night is followed by the day, and the shrill clarion of the cock proclaims the coming of the morning. Yet that crowing of the cock was to play a part in Peter's conviction. That had been given him for a sign at the Last Supper. It was not the first time, nor the last time, that a happening, a simple incident, an object even, has been used of God to speak to the soul. Even material things, because memory centers about them, may awaken deep emotions of desire or contrition. It may be a book, a picture, a child's folded dress, a jewel, a house, a room, a mountain, a river.

But the crow of the cock itself was not sufficient to work conviction of sin in Peter's heart. That was accomplished by the look of Jesus. Christ, bound, mocked, and bleeding from the blows of the officers, was being led through the hall, just when the cock crew, and just as Peter's profane oath of denial rang out on the midnight air. We are forever indebted to Luke for his account of what follows. He says that when the cock crew "the Lord turned and *looked* upon Peter"; and then it was that Peter remembered the word of the Lord, how before the cock should crow he would deny him thrice.

Angels of heaven, ye who look upon the face of Immanuel himself, can ye tell me all that was in that look of Jesus? When Othello had vented his jealous rage and anger upon the innocent Desdemona, he gazed for the last time upon her still form, saw still her dying look of pity and wounded love, and said, "This look of thine will hurl my soul from heaven." But here is the look which lifted a soul out of hell and set it in the highest heaven. In that one look of Christ there was concentrated all the past, present and future meaning of the Cross of Christ—all of its glory, its shame, its pathos, its power, and its mystery.

It was the look of wounded love; the love that looks with love upon the smiter. God spare us all that look that comes from the face of love that has been trampled upon! Yet it was also the look of appeal, of patient and ever-seeking and all forgiving love. It was the look that John Newton, the con-

PETER—WHO WAS SAVED BY A LOOK

verted slave dealer and sweet singer of the hymns, said he saw on the face of Christ on the Cross:

> "I saw One hanging on a tree,
>   In agonies and blood;
> Who fixed his languid eyes on me,
>   As near his cross I stood.
>
> "Sure, never till my latest breath,
>   Can I forget that look;
> It seemed to charge me with his death,
>   Though not a word he spoke."

It was that look of Jesus that awakened Peter, that made him realize what he had done. The look of Jesus was like a window through which Peter himself looked into the depths of his own heart.

III

PETER'S REPENTANCE

"And Peter went out, and wept bitterly." Never, I suppose, since our first parents wept at the gates of the lost Eden have such tears been shed. There are the tears that are shed over the wrongs and sufferings of mankind; and there are the tears of the lover or the maid upon whom the tragedy of life has fallen. And there are the tears that are shed over the deathbed of innocence and beauty; but the Bible makes man weep over sin; and these are the saddest of tears. Those tears of Peter are the ultimate, high-water mark expression of the pathos and sadness of sin. Listen! In many a home tonight, in many a chamber hall, in many a heart, I hear the echo of those sobs of Peter.

Dark, dark was that night into which Peter went out to weep bitterly, but there were two stars that shone for Peter that night. One was that look on the face of Jesus; the other was the memory of Christ's prayer for him, how he had said, "I have prayed for thee that thy faith fail not." Anyone who has been prayed for ought not to despair. And who has not? There are the prayers that another offered on your behalf, a godly mother, a loving wife, or a sister, a praying father. There are your own prayers that in the unclouded days of childhood's happiness and innocence you offered for yourself. But above and beyond all those prayers, is the prayer that Christ makes for you. Even if those who love you have ceased to pray for you, even if you have long since ceased to pray for yourself, remember that Christ has prayed for you. He says, "I who suffered, I who shed my blood for thee on the cross, I have prayed for thee that thy faith fail not."

And Christ's prayer for Peter was answered. Peter's faith did not fail. Satan thought he had Peter; and he almost did have him, when he persuaded him to follow afar off, and then take his seat by the fire among the enemies of Christ, and then again and again deny that he even knew his Lord. Satan thought that he had put out the light of Peter's soul in the bitterness of his grief, and had sunk him in the hell of his shame and self-condemnation. But Peter's faith did not fail! Faith in what? Faith in that into which the angels desire to look; faith in that mystery hid from the foundations of the world; faith in that which creates and maintains the church; faith in the measureless, forgiving, redeeming, cleansing, restoring power of Christ.

Yes, Satan desired to have Peter, and he almost had him. But the prayer of Christ was too much for Satan. The prayer and the look of Jesus have won the battle. Satan has lost. Now, Peter, go forth to strengthen thy brethren, as thou dost here tonight, as thou wilt do to the remotest age; more than David even—yes, more than great Paul, and more than great John, telling men and showing them how Christ is able to save, even unto the uttermost!

VI

ABRAHAM—THE MAN WHO PASSED THROUGH THE GREATEST TRIAL

> "By faith Abraham, when he was tried, offered up Isaac."
>
> HEBREWS 11:17

OVER HERE, ON THIS SIDE, UNDER THE ROOF OF THE mosque at Hebron, are the cenotaphs of the three patriarchs, Abraham, Isaac, and Jacob; not the tombs, but their monuments, or cenotaphs. Each one is covered with gorgeous green brocade, and each is shielded by a silver grille. In the middle of the floor is a circular opening, covered with a grating. From this grating a lamp is suspended. Looking down through the opening, you can see the lamp burning in the darkness far below.

You are looking into the cave of Machpelah, and there rests the dust of Abraham, Isaac, and Jacob. The wind of the ages seems to be blowing there, and you seem to hear the voice of the remotest past. You are standing where Abraham bought the Cave of Machpelah to bury his dead out of his sight. There he buried Sarah; there he himself was laid to rest; and there Isaac and Jacob were gathered to their fathers. On all the earth is there an authentic sepulcher which evokes such memories as this one

ABRAHAM—PASSED THROUGH GREATEST TRIAL

beneath the mosque at Hebron? After the death of Blaise Pascal, the great French mathematician, philosopher, and theologian, there was found sewed on his doublet a paper upon which he had written these words: "God of Abraham, God of Isaac, God of Jacob, not of philosophers and scholars, God of Jesus Christ; my God and thy God. Thy God shall be my God."

It is that thought that moves and stirs one mightily when one looks down into the Cave of Machpelah—the God of Abraham, the God of Isaac and the God of Jacob is our God, too; the same yesterday, today, and forever.

I

THE GREATNESS AND INFLUENCE OF ABRAHAM

In the sermon on Moses I said that the three greatest men of the Bible, because of the influence which they exerted and the results of their life and work, are Abraham, Moses, and Paul. But Abraham is in a certain sense, although not the noblest of them, the greatest of them, because he stands at the beginning. The spring or fountain from which a river flows is more important than any other part of the river. Abraham is the fountain whence flows the stream of faith in God. The great work of faith and redemption, God's great plan for the ages, commenced with Abraham, when God called him out of Ur of Chaldee and made him the father of the faithful and the founder of the Hebrew race. He told Abraham that in him all nations of the earth would be blessed. That prophecy, to a degree, has been fulfilled today, for all mankind have been blessed by the revelation of God given to Israel and the fulfillment of that revelation in Jesus Christ. Abraham is revered by more people of different faith and race than any other man in the Bible. The Jews venerate him as the Father of the Faithful; the Moslems venerate him as their ancestor through his son Ishmael; and the Christians venerate him as the Friend of God and the type of redeeming faith in Christ, for Christ said that Abraham rejoiced to see his day.

Abraham was by no means a perfect character. There were sad weaknesses and gross transgressions in the life of Abraham which were totally wanting in the life and character of Moses and Paul. This great man was, alas, only human. In Egypt, and afterward in Gerar, he stooped to a mean and cowardly falsehood in order to protect himself, and tried to pass off his wife as his sister. But the general trend of Abraham's life was Godward, and all succeeding prophets and representatives of God look back to Abraham and appeal to him as the Father of the Faithful.

ABRAHAM—PASSED THROUGH GREATEST TRIAL

If there are a few flaws and transgressions in Abraham's life, we must remember the age in which he lived and the magnificent witness which, in spite of these transgressions, he made to God and to the unseen world. We might speak of the call of Abraham, how he went out from his own country not knowing whither he went; and when he arrived at the Land of Promise did not possess enough of it to make even a grave for his dead. So he wandered on from place to place, but wherever he went building an altar to God and confessing that he was a pilgrim and a stranger on this earth, and that he looked for a better country, even the heavenly. "Wherefore God was not ashamed to be called his God."

Abraham was one of the great interceders of the Bible, and we might dwell on his noble intercession in behalf of the doomed cities of the plain. But we shall take Abraham at the great climax of his life, at the great trial of his life, and at the great demonstration of his faith, the greatest demonstration of faith that the world had seen until God offered up his own Son upon Calvary. "By faith Abraham, when he was tried, offered up Isaac: and he that had received the promises offered up his only begotten son." Let us look now at that great trial; let us climb the slopes of Mount Moriah and see Abraham in this supreme hour.

II

ABRAHAM'S TRIAL

"And it came to pass after these things, that God did tempt Abraham." He tempted him in the same way in which he tempts or tries you and me. God never tempts anyone to do evil, for "God cannot be tempted with evil, neither tempteth he any man." But he does tempt us to do good. He does try us to see what is in our heart. Job was greatly tried and tested of God. Some might even say that Job, and not Abraham, was the most severely tried man of the Bible. But you will note this difference between the trial of Job and the trial of Abraham: Job's trials came upon him from without. He had no choice. Hostile tribes drove off his flocks and herds and camels. The whirlwind beat down his house and killed his sons. Disease broke out in his body and drove him to the ash heap and made him curse the day he was born. But in the case of Abraham it was different. He was called upon to be the instrument and agent of his own trial and distress. He himself must strike the blow.

God had been testing Abraham's faith all through his life; but now came the supreme test, the end of his probation. God would find out in this trial if Abraham really feared him and believed in him. As

ABRAHAM—PASSED THROUGH GREATEST TRIAL

in the case of Job, God would discover if Abraham served God for nought.

It is evening at the oaks of Mamre. Evening in the Near East is always the delightful time of day. The yellow hills and sandy plains take on a soft and friendly color when night comes down, and the cool south wind begins to blow softly, refreshing the soul of man and the life of beasts. Abraham sits before the black tents meditating on the past, the way God has led him, thinking of the future and of the great promises that have been made to him. When he looks up to the star-spangled sky he remembers what God had said: "Look now toward heaven, and tell the stars, if thou be able to number them. . . . . So shall thy seed be." For a long time Abraham had wondered how that would come to pass, for the years were going by, and both he and Sarah were declining into old age. And then the wonderful thing happened, and Isaac, the Child of the Promise, through whom these great predictions were to be fulfilled, was born. There he is now, reclining before the tents, strong, handsome, robust, and virile.

When Abraham heard the voice of God, how did he know it was the voice of God? We read in this early age how God spoke to Abraham and to Moses, and to Joshua and to the prophets, and we wonder just how he spoke. How did they know that God was speaking? If that sometimes troubles us, certainly that natural and free intercourse ought to have been true at the beginning of man's history, and we know it will again be true when we shall see no longer through the glass darkly, but face to face.

But what a word is this which Abraham now hears God speaking to him! It was not concerning the greatness of the destiny of the race which was to spring from his loins. It was not concerning the starlike multitude who should constitute his seed. It was not concerning the blessing which he would bestow on all mankind. That was the way God's voice had spoken to Abraham in times past, but now it is altogether different. Not the fulfillment of the promise, but its frustration; not the multiplication of his seed, but its annihilation; not the blessing which was to fall upon mankind, but its removal. This was the word he heard the Lord speaking to him: "Take now thy son, thine only son Isaac, whom thou lovest, and get thee into the land of Moriah; and offer him there for a burnt offering upon one of the mountains which I will tell thee of."

Isaac! Sarah's son! The Son of the Promise! Isaac, through whom a blessing is to come to the remotest age, take him, offer him up for a burnt offering on the mountain top! It must have seemed to Abraham as if the earth yawned and reeled beneath his feet, as if the very stars, which were the

ABRAHAM—PASSED THROUGH GREATEST TRIAL

symbol of the greatness and multitude of the future blessing, were falling out of heaven.

All that the inspired record tells us is that in the morning Abraham arose and did as the Lord commanded. But I sometimes wonder how that long night passed with Abraham, and what thoughts and hopes and fears passed through his mind. It was not the moral problem that troubled Abraham, for in that day the father had absolute right of life and death over his son. It was a common custom in the world in which Abraham had been brought up to make a religious sacrifice of one's own offspring. It was not that which shocked Abraham, as it would you and me. His shock was emotional—his love for this handsome youth, Isaac, child of his old age. But even more than that, what troubled Abraham about this command was that Isaac was the Child of the Promise, that it was through him, and through him alone, that the great blessings to mankind in future ages were to flow. And now Abraham was told to offer him up on the mount! Why had the Lord given them this child in their old age, if he was to be offered up and taken from them? Why had God spoken to him the great promises, if now they are to be frustrated and recalled?

But when the morning came Abraham had fought his battle through and was ready to do God's will. He told Sarah and Isaac that he was going afar off to Mount Moriah to make an offering. There was the bustle and stir of great preparation as they got ready for the journey. Isaac ran about helping the servants to gather the wood and saddle the ass and fill the water vessel, and make other preparations for the expedition. Like every boy, he was eager for a trip with his father. What man here today cannot remember the thrill he had when his father took him on a trip, and how he could hardly sleep the night before in eager and restless anticipation. So it was with Isaac that morning. At length breakfast was over and the fond Sarah drew Isaac to her breast, while Abraham looked in the other direction, and kissed him goodbye. Abraham must have thought to himself, "What would Sarah have to say, if she knew where I am taking Isaac!"

On the third day they saw on the horizon the dim outline of the mountains about the Jerusalem of a later age, and soon they were at the base of Mount Moriah. Abraham told the servants to stay at the foot of the mountain with the ass while he and his son went to the mountain to worship. The bundle of faggots for the fire was laid upon Isaac's back, and Abraham carried the knife and the tinder with which to start the fire. So they went up the mountain, stopping every now and then so that the aged Abraham could rest and get his breath. When they were halfway up, and were taking one of the peri-

ABRAHAM—PASSED THROUGH GREATEST TRIAL

odic rests, Isaac said to his father, "My father, ... Behold the fire and the wood: but where is the lamb for a burnt offering?" Did ever father hear such a question from his son? Did ever father hide the hard truth from his questioning child with a more tender or more beautiful answer than Abraham gave there to Isaac: "My son, God will provide himself a lamb for a burnt offering"?

Isaac wondered how that could be; but he had learned to trust his father and had learned to trust in God; so he asked no further questions. Together they gathered the stones and built the altar and put the wood in order upon the altar. But still there was no sign of the lamb for the offering, and Isaac began to wonder what it all meant. Then Abraham told him the truth. The boy himself was to be the lamb for the offering. If this was an exhibition of supreme faith on the part of Abraham, how beautiful an instance it was of supreme faith and unquestioning submission on the part of Isaac. Had he so minded, with his strong robust arm he might have seized the knife out of Abraham's hand and smitten him there at the altar. But Isaac, whose meekness and submission are always a type of Christ, permitted himself to be bound on the altar. Like Christ, as the prophet described him, "He opened not his mouth."

Then Abraham seized the knife and poised it aloft, its silver blade flashing in the bright Syrian sunlight. But ere the knife could fall, Abraham heard a voice out of heaven, "Lay not thine hand upon the lad, neither do thou anything unto him: for now I know that thou fearest God, seeing thou hast not withheld thy son, thine only son from me." At that same moment Abraham saw a ram struggling in the thicket, and quickly cutting the cords that bound Isaac, together they seized the ram and offered it upon the altar. How gladly and happily the father and son must have descended the mountain that day, and how pleasant to both of them was the homeward journey, and how delighted they were to see the black tents again by the oaks of Mamre and to receive the greeting of Sarah.

Abraham had stood the terrible test. To all intents and purposes, he had offered up his only son on the altar. God knew that Abraham feared him and believed in him, "Now I know that thou fearest God, seeing thou hast not withheld thy son, thine only son from me." That was the end of Abraham's probation. He had been tried and not found wanting. Now God repeated the blessing. It was no longer a hypothetical blessing, but one which was assured. The faith of Abraham guaranteed the blessing. God said to him, "Because thou hast done this thing, and hast not withheld thy son, thine only son: that in blessing I will bless thee, and in multiplying I will multiply thy seed as the stars of the heaven, and as the sand which is upon the sea shore; .... and in thy seed shall all the nations of the earth be blessed, because thou hast obeyed my voice." Think of that! All humanity, to the remotest age, forever blessed because there on the mount one man obeyed God!

Abraham called the mount where the great trial took place, "Jehovah-jireh," "The Lord will provide." Forever to tried and suffering souls that mount where Abraham offered up Isaac will repeat that precious and blessed truth, "The Lord will provide." That was what he said to the wondering Isaac as they toiled up the mountain when Isaac wanted to know where the lamb was for the sacrifice. What can we do but submit to God's will, obey his commands and trust where we cannot see? We have far better assurance than Abraham had, for we have the assurance of God's love given to us in Christ, his own Son, offered up for us on the cross. That lets us know that we can trust God and wait upon him.

"If called like Abraham's child to climb
   Some hill of sacrifice;
 Some angel may be there in time,
   Deliverance shall arise." [1]

If God spared not his own Son but offered him

---
[1] Wm. J. Irons.

upon the cross for us, will he not freely give us all things?

It is easier, of course, to talk about Abraham and to praise him than to emulate him, to do as Abraham did, to trust in God as he trusted in God. What shall we do? What will you do in your hour of trial? God may ask you to lay on the altar your ambition, your affection, your earthly hope, your earthly delight, the strength of your body, the ambition of the mind. Yes, like Abraham, the one you love the most. Will you be able to do it? How much will your faith be able to stand? Will you be able to say with Abraham, "The Lord will provide"? Or with Job, "Though he slay me, yet will I trust in him"? In this supreme moment of his life Abraham shows us what faith can accomplish, to how much it can submit.

Here is the man who blessed mankind more than any other who came into the world until Christ himself came and died on that other mount near Moriah. And how did Abraham do it? Not in words that he wrote, not in cities or towns that he built, not in any great accomplishment, as the world counts accomplishment, but in what he gave up, in what he offered to let go. Perhaps thus, and in ways that we know not how, God will use our obedience, our faith, our trust in him to bless mankind. Oh, be sure of that! No one holds fast to God for himself

ABRAHAM—PASSED THROUGH GREATEST TRIAL

but he helps bind some other close to God. This is the greatest thing that God can do with any soul. This is the greatest thing that any soul can do for God: to show that it loves him and trusts him to the uttermost.

And God still comes to see, to discover, if we really trust him. When our time comes, when the voice bids us climb Mount Moriah's rocky slope, shall we be able to follow in the footsteps of Abraham? Will God be able to say of us, "Now I know that thou fearest me"? God wants to know that above all else, and God sends his Son to bear our sins on the Cross, to testify to his love for us, that we might give him our love and our faith; that we might answer God's great "I know" with our own "I know," the "I know" of St. Paul—"I know whom I have believed, and am persuaded that he is able to keep that which I have committed unto him against that day."

VII

JOSEPH—DREAMS, DUNGEONS, DIADEMS

"Behold, this dreamer cometh."
GENESIS 37:19

SPRINGTIME ON THE PLAIN OF DOTHAN, IN THE Vale of Esdraelon. To the south the mountains of Samaria; to the north the mountains of Gilboa. Standing on one of the lower ranges of the bordering mountains, we see black dots against the green grass of the plain. These are the black tents of the sons of Jacob who are feeding their flocks on the Plain of Dothan. And yonder are white dots. These are flocks of sheep against the green of the plain, like lingering snow on a March day. But away yonder, coming from the south with greetings from his father for his brethren, is Joseph, his coat of many colors brushing the dews from the lips of the spring flowers as he walks across the plain.

Love can see afar off; and so can hate. The father of the prodigal saw the returning son when he was "yet a great way off," and Joseph's brethren saw him "afar off." When they saw him they said one to another, with hatred in their voice and envy in their eyes, "Behold, this dreamer cometh!"

JOSEPH—DREAMS, DUNGEONS, DIADEMS

The world loves a dreamer. That is one reason for the popularity of Joseph, and why, in the vote of the congregation he takes seventh place among the great men of the Bible. The world's greatest story centers about the world's greatest dreamer. Forever this will be the story for young men and young women, for it has in it all the elements of life's great story—ambition, dreams, hope, love, sorrow, envy, hate, temptation, lust, vengeance, suffering, sorrow, sin and conquest. The popularity of Joseph shows how, after all, the great things of life do not change. The things of the heart and of the soul are the same from age to age. The world loves Joseph, too, because he was a great sufferer. Sorrow and suffering and hardship are deepest graven on the history of men. They have a deeper appeal than pleasure and ease and plenty. Joseph was the great dreamer; but because of his dreams he was also the great sufferer.

I

DREAMS

"Behold, this dreamer cometh!" Yes, behold the dreamer; for when you look at him you behold one of the secrets of achievement. Joseph has extraordinary dreams. In one dream he saw the sheaves of his brothers bowing down to his sheaf when they were binding sheaves in the field. And in another dream he saw the sun and the moon and the eleven stars, the number of his brethren, doing obeisance to him. Joseph's brothers hated him for his dreams, and for his words of naive assurance as to his future; and even doting Jacob pretended to rebuke him for his dreams; but secretly, I am sure, he was as proud of the dreams of Joseph as he was fond of him.

Joseph's dreams were not crude, arrogant, and selfish dreams. They were sacramental; they had to do with the beauty and greatness of life. To dream true, to hitch one's wagon to a star, is the first equipment for the battle of life. General Grant as a cadet at West Point hated the army, and when a bill was pending in Congress for the dissolution of the Academy, the young cadet eagerly read the newspapers hoping that he would find that the Academy had been abolished. But one day he saw Winfield Scott, the Lieutenant General of the Army, and the hero of two wars, ride by in a review at West Point, and when he saw that, he thought to himself, "How wonderful it would be if I one day were in Scott's place." Thus even the homesick cadet, weary with his military drill and duties, had his dream of future distinction.

Our dreams are the golden ladder by which we climb to heavenly places. They are the mountain peaks of vision whence we see afar off the country towards which we travel. They are the lantern by whose light we pass safely through dark valleys. They are the inner flame that gives us strength and energy for the struggle. They are the two-edged sword by which we cleave the steaming head of the dragon of temptation, and leave him dying at our feet.

"Behold, this dreamer cometh." One of the most famous American politicians of the last century a few days before his death said to a friend, that when he was dead the newspapers would say that a political boss was dead; but had he lived his life differently they would have spoken of his death as the death of a statesman. "Take warning by me, young man," he said to the young senator to whom he was talking. Then, taking up a book, he wrote on the flyleaf the enigmatic words, "Dream true," and gave them to his friend as a parting gift.

II

DUNGEONS

"Behold, this dreamer cometh." But sometimes the saying must be, "Behold, this dreamer *goeth*," for the dreamer has forsaken his dream.

Dreams invite the attack of the world. When they saw him afar off that morning, the brothers of Joseph said, "Behold, this dreamer cometh! Come, let us kill him, and we shall see what will become of his dreams." The world, if it can, will strip a man of his dreams. It will attack him with sorrow and suffering and temptation, and loneliness, and hatred, and envy, and disappointment, and then wait to see what will come of his dreams. In many cases, alas, nothing comes of the dreamer's dream, because, under the stress of the world's attack and temptation the dream is abandoned, forsaken, betrayed, and sold for a mess of pottage. Is not that the sorrow and tragedy of many a life? Let many a man today face himself as he was in college, ten, twenty, fifty years ago, and then tell me what has become of his dreams.

The world seeks not only to make a man forget or forsake his dreams, or unwilling to make the sacrifice required for their fulfillment, but to make him unworthy of his dreams. That is the saddest disaster of all, when a man has not only forgotten and forsaken his dreams, but is unworthy of the dream that once illuminated his face and lighted his pathway in life.

But Joseph was faithful to his dreams. The world put him to a fiery trial and test. There was first the trial of envy and of hate. They intended first to kill him; but through Reuben's intervention he was cast into a pit, and it was the plan of Reuben to rescue him when he had opportunity. But Judah, not only ready for murder, but like Judas, eager to profit by it, suggested during the absence of Reuben, when a caravan of Ishmaelites hove in sight on their way down into Egypt, that they sell their brother to the Ishmaelites. The bargain was struck and Joseph was sold for twenty pieces of silver, ten less than Jesus brought on the market of hate and envy. There is Joseph, bound to the back of one of the camels of the Ishmaelites, as the caravan slowly winds its way southward. The caravan route passed not far from Hebron; and perhaps Joseph with aching heart saw far in the distance the black tents of Jacob and wondered if he would ever see them again. Yet Joseph is still the dreamer.

In Egypt, sold for a slave, he resolves to become the best and most useful and most benevolent slave in the household; with the result that all the affairs of the captain of the guard's household were put in Joseph's hands. The record is, that the "Lord blessed the Egyptian's house for Joseph's sake." A good man, a godly man, a kind man, is a blessing wherever fate, or fortune, or, as Joseph would have put it, God has placed him. Every life can be a blessing to some other life. Is that ground, that house, that office, that home, blessed or cursed for thy sake?

Joseph has survived the attack of adversity. Sold by his brothers to the Ishmaelites, and sold by the Ishmaelites to Potiphar as a slave, he is still faithful to his dreams. Now comes the fiery trial of temptation—woman. Woman has crowned many a dreamer, but many a dreamer, too, she has uncrowned. The test of temptation waits there on the pathway of life for every dreamer. Others can warn you and pray for you and hope for you, but you alone are the battler, you alone can act in the presence of the tempter. Who shall command the battle? Thou! The best your friends can do is to impress upon the mind of youth the fact that this enemy must be faced, that this battle must be fought, and all that is to come afterwards—influence, inward peace and respect, joy, and hope—depends upon the issue of this battle. There is no greater tragedy in life than the tragedy of those who have yielded to *just one* temptation, but thereby disqualified themselves to serve the dream of life.

But Joseph stood the test; and the longer the stretch of the ages between Joseph and today, the more I wonder at Joseph's stand and the victory which he won. It was a victory won in the face of great odds. Joseph was not a shriveled Egyptian mummy, but a full-blooded Hebrew youth. There was the element of flattery, too, to which the young heart responds so easily; flattery that a great lady of the Egyptians had conceived an affection for him. There was the likelihood, too, of promotion, with such a powerful friend at court as Potiphar's wife. There was the consideration, too, that if he did not yield he would be, as he soon was, the victim of revenge, for "Hell hath no fury like a woman scorned." Then Joseph was only a slave, and slaves were not supposed to have morals. He was far from home, too, and the God of Jacob had not saved him from slavery in Egypt. Why, then, should he be true to him? Yet, Joseph stood firm.

And how did he win his victory? What sword was it that Joseph wielded in this dread hour? His sword is preserved for us in the museum of the Book of Genesis. You can still read the inscription cut upon the sword that Joseph wielded; and this is the inscription," How shall I do this great evil and sin against God?" With that sword Joseph won his immortal victory. The Jews have a tradition that just when Joseph was about to yield to the temptress, the vision of the face of Jacob his father rose before him, and when he thought of Jacob he was saved from surrender and shame. But what does that legend embody? It means that the sight of the face of Jacob was to Joseph as the sight of the face of God. When he thought of God Joseph said, "How can I do this great evil and sin against God?" He pronounced that most difficult word to pronounce in all languages—Egyptian, Hebrew, Greek, French, German, English, Choctaw—and that word is "No!" When the angels, the seraphim and the cherubim, heard that "No" of Joseph's echo in heaven, they took up their harps and smote them into grand music, for there is joy among the angels of heaven over one soul who says "No" to the tempter.

Joseph's victory put him where many a victory over temptation for the sake of principle has put a man—in prison. A woman's vengeance and a false and wicked accusation landed him in the dungeon. I have sometimes wondered how Joseph felt that first night in the prison, and what he said to himself that first night. Did a voice whisper to him, "Joseph, does it pay to dream? Does it pay to be true to your dreams? Instead of lying in this stinking dungeon you might have been out in the bright Egyptian sunlight, on your way to fame and prosperity in the land of Egypt. Do you think it pays to be true to your dreams?" But Joseph, I am sure, answered the tempter, "Yes, it pays. This dungeon is dark, but I can lighten its darkness with the lantern of a good conscience."

In the dungeon Joseph still hopes and believes, loves and dreams. His kindness and optimism do not fail him. If he must be in prison, he is determined to be the best, the most hopeful, the most cheerful, the most helpful prisoner in all the prison. He can interpret the dreams of other men because he has been true to his own dream. Only the faithful dreamer can do that. The only time that Joseph came near to breaking down was when after he had interpreted the dream of the chief butler, and the interpretation had come true, and the chief butler was leaving the prison, Joseph, in tears, besought him not to forget him, but to remember him and make mention of him at the court of Pharaoh. Then the door closed again and Joseph was left alone in the dungeon. The years passed by, yet did not that most human chief butler remember Joseph, but forgot him. Did the voice whisper again to Joseph, "Joseph, does it pay to be true to your dreams? You might have been out in the sunlight, a free man, like the chief butler who long ago has forgotten you, if you had only yielded to the tempter"? But still Joseph is the dreamer, and still he is true to his dream.

III

DIADEMS

Dreams, then dungeons, but at last the diadem! When Pharaoh could not interpret his strange dreams of the full ears and thin ears, and the fat cattle and the thin cattle, the chief butler finally remembered Joseph, and mentioned him to Pharaoh, and Joseph was brought out of the dungeon to interpret the dream of the king; and this in turn led to his promotion to the first place in Egypt after Pharaoh. He wore Pharaoh's ring on his hand, and Pharaoh's robe on his back, and Pharaoh's gold chain about his neck, and had for his wife the daughter of the sacred priest of On.

Had this story been written by a secular penman, or if some romancer had written it, it would have come to a conclusion there. But that is not where the divine penman stopped. In many respects the greatest chapter in this story of Joseph is the final chapter.

Prosperity sometimes makes men forget God. Sometimes it makes them hard and cruel. Sometimes it makes them forget old friends. But not so Joseph. Great in the dreams of youth, great in the adversities and trials through which he had passed, great in the hour of temptation, Joseph is greatest of all in his prosperity, when his dreams have come true.

He never forgot his father's house. Sometimes when he was handling his great business for Pharaoh, the lords and officers would ask him a question, and Joseph would not answer. He had not heard the question. He was hearing the voice of Jacob, the voice of Benjamin. Sometimes when he was sitting at ease in his palace, a look of abstraction would come over his countenance, and his wife, the daughter of the priest of On, would shake him by the arm, and ask him if he had forgotten her; or she would place Ephraim on one knee and Manasseh on the other knee, and tell him to call home his wander-

JOSEPH—DREAMS, DUNGEONS, DIADEMS

ing thoughts and think of her and of his sons. But Joseph's thoughts were far away from that beautiful palace. He saw not the red sandstone columns twined about with serpents, and surmounted by great eagles in whose eyes and in whose talons flashed precious stones. He saw not the far off winding Nile, nor the huge Pyramids, nor the silent staring Sphinx. Joseph's thoughts were far away from Egypt, at the black tents of Hebron, for,

" 'Mid pleasures and palaces though we may roam,
Be it ever so humble there's no place like home.
. . . .
An exile from home, splendor dazzles in vain,
Oh, give me my lowly thatched cottage again." [1]

And as he thought of that home in Canaan, Joseph would say to himself, "Doth my father still live? And Benjamin, is he alive? And the ten cruel brothers who sold me into Egypt?" Joseph dreams of reunion. And that dream, too, came true.

One day, when the famine was sore in Israel, Joseph's brethren appeared before him to buy corn. The years have disguised Joseph to them, but the years could never disguise his brothers to Joseph. After probing their conscience and arousing their fears, Joseph at length disclosed himself unto them; and as they wept together, tears of repentance on the

[1] John Howard Payne.

part of his brothers, tears of affection and forgiveness on the part of Joseph, a scene which will be matched only when all the redeemed and forgiven meet their Saviour and Redeemer in heaven, and look upon him whom they have pierced, all the Egyptians heard them weeping. Then comes the greatest act of Joseph's noble life. When his brethren feared that he would take vengeance upon them after their father was dead, he tells them that they need have no fear, that he does not stand in the place of God. As for them, they meant evil against him, but God meant it unto good. It was the divine plan for the saving alive of Israel. If Joseph had not been sold into Egypt, if he had not resisted the temptation of Potiphar's wife, if he had not been cast into the dungeon, if he had not been forgotten for so long a time by the chief butler, he would never have reached his high post in the land of Pharaoh and would never have been able to save Jacob and his family and the Israel of God from starvation.

The long series of trials, his dreams, his dungeons, his diadems, had taught Joseph the doctrine of providence. God meant it unto good. Joseph was a link in the long chain of redemption, and therefore we may say that Christ in his work depended upon Joseph. Joseph is able now to bless every circumstance in his life, his cruel brothers, the Ishmaelites,

Potiphar's wife, the jailer in the prison, the chief butler who forgot him, for each one played a necessary part in the drama of his life, which was to result in the saving alive of his father's house.

Here is a deep comment, too, on the meaning of life, how all must be related to the end, and how we cannot pass judgment until we see the end. Who would have dreamed that that young Hebrew lad, bound to the camel's back as it went swaying down with the Ishmaelites into Egypt, or the lad who was cast into the Egyptian dungeon on a cruel charge was, in the providence of God, to be the deliverer of his people! The experience of Joseph tells us that the world is a vale of soul-making, that this life is a probation, the end and purpose of which is to develop and exercise spiritual and moral qualities in the soul with a view to their coronation in the world to come.

"Behold, this dreamer cometh!" Yes, Joseph, come again into our midst! Put that ring of constancy upon thy finger, and that robe woven by thine own fidelity and obedience. Hang again about thy neck that gold chain forged out of the furnace of thy fiery trials. Walk down our streets. Enter our places of amusement. Pass through our business offices. Enter the cloisters of our colleges and universities. Pass down the aisles of our churches, and tell us once more, as thou alone art able to tell, that duty is the pathway to glory; that our dreams light the way sometimes to suffering, but in the end to victory; that it is Christlike ever to forgive; that forever it pays to be true to our dreams; and that by our fidelity to God and our loyalty to principle we join the company of those prophets, apostles, and martyrs, who from age to age have pushed forward the boundaries of the Kingdom of God.

When thou wast dying, Joseph, thou saidst, "Bury me not in Egypt," for although it came long centuries afterwards, thou hadst faith that the people of God would be brought again into the promised land; and when they came they brought thy dust with them. No, Joseph, thou wast not buried in Egypt! Thou art forever enshrined in the hearts of men who love the truth and serve God. The ages cannot bury thee. Time cannot engulf thee. As thou didst bless of old the house of Potiphar, so to the remotest age thou shalt bless and cheer and help the sons of men.

VIII

ISAIAH—THE MAN WHO SAW CHRIST'S GLORY

> "And there was delivered unto him the book of the prophet Esaias."
>
> Luke 4:17

THAT CERTAINLY WAS A MOST APPROPRIATE BEGINning to the ministry and preaching of Christ. After his temptation Jesus returned in the power of the Spirit to Galilee and came to Nazareth where he was brought up. As his custom was, he went into the synagogue on the Sabbath day, and was invited by the elders to read the lesson for the day. "And there was delivered unto him the book of the prophet Isaiah." The lesson for the day, and the part that he read, was that beautiful prophetic passage from Isaiah's sixty-first chapter: "The Spirit of the Lord God is upon me; because the Lord hath anointed me to preach good tidings unto the meek; he hath sent me to bind up the brokenhearted, to proclaim liberty to the captives, and the opening of the prison to them that are bound; to proclaim the acceptable year of the Lord."

Almost any other passage from Isaiah would have done as well, for the whole Book of Isaiah is radiant with the glory of Christ. John said of Isaiah, after relating how Jesus had quoted him to the scribes and Pharisees, "These things said Isaiah, when he saw his glory and spake of him." No one ever saw more of the glory of Christ, not even Abraham who saw his day and rejoiced; nor Moses who wrote of him; nor David who sang of him; nor Peter, nor Paul, nor John, who saw him standing in the midst of the seven golden candlesticks in the Isle of Patmos. More than any one of them, more than all of them together, Isaiah saw his glory and spake of him. In the apocryphal book, the Ascension of Isaiah, it is related how when the prophet was talking with King Hezekiah he was suddenly carried away by an angel. He traveled the firmament and witnessed the battle of the angels and the demons between the earth and the moon. He entered and passed through the six heavens and saw all their glory. Then he ascended to the seventh heaven itself, where he looked upon the Holy Trinity and beheld all the events of futurity pass in review before him.

The legend of the apocryphal book is only a legend; but it expresses a great truth, and that is that all the glory of the heavenly places, the glory of the prophets and the apostles, the angels and the martyrs, the glory of the Father, Son, and Holy Ghost, and the future glory of the Kingdom of God, is reflected in the pages of Isaiah's book. Once I took a red pencil when reading through Isaiah and thought to

ISAIAH—WHO SAW CHRIST'S GLORY

mark, as I passed from chapter to chapter, those verses or passages which were of striking beauty, marvelous sublimity, or tender and appealing pathos. But as I drew near to the end of the book I came to the conclusion that the best plan would be to take my red pencil and draw a circle around the entire book, for on every page there is glory. There are sixty-six chapters in the book of Isaiah, just as there are sixty-six books in the Bible. That is just a coincidence. But it is an undoubted fact that the Book of Isaiah is, as it were, a summary and compendium of all the books of the Bible. When Jesus and the evangelists and the apostles and Paul quote from their Bible, the Old Testament, it is almost always the Book of Isaiah from which they quote. Our Lord began his ministry with a sermon in the synagogue at Nazareth, when he took for his text the words of Isaiah, "The Spirit of the Lord God is upon me, because the Lord hath anointed me to preach good tidings unto the meek; he hath sent me to bind up the brokenhearted"; and although on the cross Jesus seems to quote a verse from the twenty-second psalm, his last direct citation from the Old Testament was on the night of his betrayal, when he quoted a verse from the fifty-third chapter of Isaiah, "He was numbered with the transgressors," and said that that night the prophecy would be fulfilled in him.

The last recorded utterance of Paul as a preacher

is a quotation from the Book of Isaiah; and the noblest passages in Paul—and that is saying a great deal—come from the pages of Isaiah. Such as: "Now is the acceptable time, now is the day of salvation"; "Eye hath not seen nor ear heard, neither have entered into the mind of man the things which God has prepared for them that love him"; and that great shout at the end of the great chapter on mortality, "O Death, where is thy sting! O Grave, where is thy victory!" In the Apocalypse of John some of the grandest and sweetest music, the softly flowing river of water of life, the compassionate God wiping away all tears from our eyes, and the glorious City where the gates are never shut and the sun never goes down—all that comes from Isaiah.

One of the great joys in heaven, I am sure, will be the joy of listening to the great preachers hold forth on the love and majesty of God. What an experience that will be, to hear Moses one day, and Jeremiah the next, and John the Baptist the next, and Peter the next, and then John, and then Paul! But when the seventh day comes, I imagine the preacher for the day by universal consent will be Isaiah; and we shall see those great preachers I have named, and all the prophets and the apostles, even Peter, John, and Paul, sitting at the feet of Isaiah and listening to him, for all that they said he said

ISAIAH—WHO SAW CHRIST'S GLORY

long before their day. "He saw his glory, and spake of him."

Yet the strange thing is, that of this great prophet and preacher we know almost nothing. He hides himself behind his great Christ, even more successfully than does John in his Gospel. Only once or twice is the curtain lifted on Isaiah's personal life: once when he saw the glory of God in the temple in the reign of King Uzziah; and again when in the days of King Hezekiah he pronounced the judgment of God upon the blasphemous Sennacherib, when the angel of the Lord went forth and smote the proud invader and his army. But outside of that we know nothing of Isaiah. If, therefore, in the vote of the congregation Isaiah was given the eighth place among the great men of the Bible, it must have been Isaiah's book that they were voting for, and when they thought of Isaiah's book, there is no doubt that what was in their mind was that one sublime passage of his book, the fifty-third chapter. Hence, the best way to preach on Isaiah will be to preach on that great chapter.

In the history of painting there is the English school, and the Flemish school, the German school, the French school, the Russian school, the Italian school, and the Spanish school. All these different schools of painting have presented to us their conception of the Son of God. But it is in the Hebrew school that we have portrayed the Universal Christ. In this school we pass through the galleries of the Old Testament, and look upon the Christ of Moses, and David, and Jeremiah, and Malachi; and in the New Testament we see the masterpieces of the evangelists and the apostles. But there is one great painting in this gallery of the Old Testament which still attracts the greatest multitudes. When you go to the Royal Gallery in Dresden, if you follow the crowd you will soon find yourself in the little chapel where the Sistine Madonna is enshrined in her matchless charm and beauty. When you go to the Rycks Museum in Amsterdam, all you have to do is to follow the crowd, and it will soon bring you to the gallery where you can see Rembrandt's famous "Night Watch." Just follow the crowd, then, in the Old Testament gallery, and it will bring you face to face with the world's greatest painting of Christ. And there it is! And there he is! And there he hangs, upon the cross for the sins of the world, despised and rejected, the Man of Sorrows and acquainted with grief. As on the day when he died on Calvary the people and his friends "sat down and watched him there" as he died, so tonight let us sit down before this marvelous painting and watch the Son of God as he dies for us, and for the whole world.

ISAIAH—WHO SAW CHRIST'S GLORY

I

THE DESPISED AND REJECTED CHRIST

I look at this painting of Isaiah, and that is the first thing that strikes me about it. He is despised and rejected of men. "He hath no form, nor comeliness; and when we shall see him, there is no beauty that we should desire him." This is still true. Christ is rejected as to his teachings and precepts. What kingdom or state on earth is established upon those precepts? Name over the Beatitudes of Jesus, and then look for a kingdom or institution, outside of his Church, which is founded upon them. No; not one of them!

> "Our Lord is now rejected,
> And by the world disowned,
> By the many still neglected,
> And by the few enthroned." [1]

Christ is rejected, too, as a Redeemer from sin. Many speak with emotion and sentiment about the Cross of Christ; but too often it is a cross the offense of which has ceased. It is a cross in which there is no condemnation for sin, and no substitution of Christ in the sinner's place. He is praised often as a prophet and inspirer and friend and teacher, but still despised as a Redeemer. For the majority of

---

[1] Author unknown.

people, there is no beauty in Christ. "When we shall see him, there is no beauty that we should desire him." And here, too, is the pathos, and bitterness, of self-accusation: "We hid as it were our faces from him; he was despised, and we esteemed him not." Alas! how true that has often been! We esteemed the world more than Christ, and before the world and its power, and passion, and wealth, and pleasure, we were ashamed of the Man of Sorrows. "We hid as it were our faces from him." Oh, the shame of being ashamed of Christ!

II

THE MAN OF SORROWS

I look once more at this sublime painting, and what strikes me now is this: It shows him as the Man of Sorrows. "He was a Man of Sorrows and acquainted with grief." Sorrow is universal. Not all men know great happiness. Not all men know fame. Not all men experience persecution. But all men know sorrow. Because Christ is the Man of Sorrows, he is the Universal Christ.

He was the Man of Sorrows because he was the Creator of the world, and when he looked upon this lost, fallen, sin-stained, sin-cursed, and sin-befouled, and sin-trampled world, it was with the sorrow of him who is its Lord and Creator. It was his world.

His was the sorrow, too, of loneliness. No one on earth, not even the disciples nearest to him, could understand or sympathize with him or help him in the great work of redemption that he was to do upon the Cross. "I have trodden the winepress alone; and of the people there was none with me." His was the sorrow, too, of the despised and rejected and execrated Christ. He who came with a heart full of love was met with scorn and contempt and a chorus of scorn and mockery and execration which reached its awful climax at the cross when they mocked him and shouted, "Crucify him!"

His was the sorrow, too, of one who was betrayed, forsaken, and abandoned by his friends. One sold him for thirty pieces of silver. Another, and the closest to him, denied with an oath that he had ever known him. Yes, of a truth, "He was a Man of Sorrows and acquainted with grief." But that very fact draws us to him, for it is the Man of Sorrow himself who hath carried our sorrows and borne our griefs. And he alone could have done it.

III

THE SINNER'S SUBSTITUTE

And this brings me to the next great fact about the Christ of this painting. I look once more at Isaiah's masterpiece, and what I see now is the Sinner's Substitute. I see one who was numbered with the transgressors; I see one who was wounded for our transgressions and bruised for our iniquities. "The Lord hath laid on him the iniquity of us all."

That is what I see now as I look at Isaiah's Christ. I see one upon whom God hath laid the iniquity of us all. That was in view of the fact that all we like sheep have gone astray. Perhaps a man rises now and says, "Wait; I see yonder a man who cheated another in a business deal. I see yonder another who sings the hymns heartily, but who neglects his wife and his family. I see yonder another who takes up an evil tale against his neighbor. And over there I see a profane swearer; and over yonder one who has betrayed innocence. When you say, 'All we like sheep have gone astray,' when you speak of 'the iniquity of us all,' I suppose it is persons like that you mean."

No; that is not what I mean. I mean *all* of us. "All we like sheep have gone astray." When sheep go astray they never find themselves. The shepherd must go out and find them and bring them back to the fold, else they must perish. Christ, the great Shepherd of God, came to seek and to save the lost sheep. How strange and wonderful and awful was that way in which he saved us. He was smitten of God! The Lord laid upon him the iniquity of us all.

He put him to grief. He made his soul an offering for sin. How can you explain that? I cannot explain it. The angels themselves cannot explain it; but it was God's way. "He hath put him to grief." No wonder the sun in heaven hid his face and the earth rocked and groaned in amazement when Christ was made an offering for sin and poured out his soul unto death, and was numbered with the transgressors, died for you and me, with a transgressor, a wicked thief on his right hand and on his left hand. Now I begin to understand better what wicked and cruel Caiaphas, the high priest, said, that it was expedient that one man should die for the people. Now I begin to see the deeper meaning of that beautiful verse of this chapter, "Surely he hath borne our griefs, and carried our sorrows."

IV

THE TRIUMPHANT AND VICTORIOUS CHRIST

I look once more at Isaiah's painting and lo, this is what I see now, the Triumphant and Victorious Christ. How strange the transformation! Why, just a moment ago I looked, and it was all darkness and gloom. But now it is the glory of the morning! Just a moment ago I looked, and I saw him surrounded by mockers, and scorners, and persecutors, despised and rejected of men; but now I see him surrounded by a mighty throng, gathered out of every kindred, and nation, and tribe, and people, and tongue, who acclaim him as their king. Just a moment ago I looked, and all that I saw was one dying and bleeding and wounded and cursed upon a cross. But now I look, and behold, a Conqueror on a white horse, and all the armies of heaven follow him, and on his vesture and on his thigh a name is written, "King of Kings," and "Lord of Lords."

How skillful and inspired the painter must have been who can make us see that in this crucified servant of God. But that is now what we see. He is the King of Kings, and the Lord of Lords, his kingdom founded upon death and love lives and grows from age to age, while the kingdoms of this world, founded upon sin and force, follow one another into the grave of oblivion. Yes; here is the Conqueror. "Therefore will I divide him a portion with the great, and he shall divide the spoil with the strong, because He hath poured out his soul unto death." "He shall see of the travail of his soul, and shall be satisfied." Christ shall see and be satisfied with the character and with the number of all his redeemed, from that dying thief whom he took from the cross into heaven with him to the last soul who shall be brought home to God through the power of the Cross.

ISAIAH—WHO SAW CHRIST'S GLORY

All hail to the Conqueror! Standing one Fourteenth of July by the Arc de Triomphe, I saw a great French military parade. First of all came the cavalry on their beautiful chestnut horses, and then the infantry, and then the artillery, and then all the equipment and paraphernalia of war. And loud cheers went up as this great host, led by mounted musicians who played on their French horns the stirring air of the march from *Aida,* marched around the great arch inscribed with the victories of Napoleon and down the sunlit avenue. But what was that compared with that day when Christ shall see of the travail of his soul and be satisfied, when he shall take captivity captive and divide the spoils with the great?

Isaiah, his brush inspired by the Holy Spirit, did not paint this great picture just that we might admire it, but that men might be saved by it. Eighty years from tonight, at the utmost, every one in this congregation will be in eternity. Within fifty years most of you will be there. Within twenty-five years many of you. Within ten years not a few. Within one year certainly some of you. Therefore, I hold up before you Jesus Christ and him crucified. He was wounded for your sins. He was bruised for your iniquities. And the Lord hath laid on him your transgressions.

One of the earliest sermons of which we have record was preached on this chapter. The Ethiopian treasurer of the Queen of Ethiopia was on his way from Jerusalem down to Africa, and as he sat in his chariot he was looking at this painting that we have been looking at tonight, and reading these wonderful sentences of Isaiah, but hardly knowing as you are able to know, their meaning. He was joined by Philip, the Evangelist, who got up in the chariot by his side and asked him to show him what he was reading. And the Ethiopian pointed to this chapter. Philip asked him if he understood what he was reading, and the Ethiopian confessed that he did not know what it meant. The place was where it says, "He was led as a lamb to the slaughter, and as a sheep before his shearers is dumb, so he openeth not his mouth." He told Philip he did not know whether the prophet was talking about himself or some other man. And then Philip, beginning at that very place, "All we like sheep have gone astray; we have turned every one to his own way; and the Lord hath laid on him the iniquity of us all," preached Christ unto him. He made it so clear and wonderful to this foreign statesman that the one of whom Isaiah spoke was the Son of God, the Saviour of the world, that the black man said, "I want to be his disciple. I believe that he is the Son of God, that he died for me on the cross." And when he said that, the chariot was stopped, and Philip took him down into the water and baptized him. Then we read that Philip was caught up and disappeared, but that the Ethiopian "went on his way rejoicing."

I would like to send someone on his way rejoicing tonight; someone who has discovered tonight that Jesus is the great Burdenbearer; some sorrowing soul who has found out tonight that Christ is able to bear his griefs and carry his sorrows for him; some lonely soul who has found tonight a Friend who will never leave him nor forsake him; and someone who has often heard this before, that Christ was wounded for our transgressions and bruised for our iniquities, but who never before applied it to himself; someone who tonight shall confess that he is a sinner, and go on his way rejoicing with a joy that shall last through all eternity, and in which the angels, too, shall share, because he has found him whose precious blood cleanses the soul from the stain of sin. "Though your sins be as scarlet, they shall be as white as snow."

IX

ELIJAH—THE SON OF THUNDER

"Behold, Elijah is here."

I KINGS 18:8

"BEHOLD ELIJAH IS HERE." BUT WHAT OF THAT? It can be said of a vast number of people, "He is here," and it would mean little or nothing whether he was here or not. What difference would it make? The fact that they were here would not rebuke evildoers or encourage those who strive for the truth. It would not help or guide, or warn, or cheer, or comfort, or inspire any soul. But when you say, "Behold, Elijah is here," that is a different matter. Elijah is here! Therefore let idolaters beware! Let evildoers flee! Let tyrants tremble! Let the discouraged and the disheartened take courage. Let the hopeless have hope. Let all those who have not bowed the knee to Baal rejoice and give thanks. Behold, Elijah is here!

This sentence was spoken under circumstances which, like all the incidents in the life of Elijah, were most dramatic. It was three and a half years after Elijah had pronounced the judgment of the drought upon the idolatrous court and the people,

ELIJAH—THE SON OF THUNDER

and for three and a half years it had not rained. The whole land languished under the famine. The wicked King Ahab had set out in one direction through the land and his prime minister, Obadiah, who was a God-fearing man, in the other direction to search for water and for pasturage. As Obadiah was in the way, he was suddenly confronted by Elijah, who said to him, "Go tell the king, Behold, Elijah is here."

Because of who Elijah was, and the mighty Name in which he spoke, to say, "Elijah is here," means that there is the power and the presence of God in the life of men and in the life of nations.

I

THE COMFORT AND THE KINDNESS OF GOD

To say, "Elijah is here," means that we have the comfort and the presence of God in the hour of our trial and sorrow. On one occasion our Lord took the disciples apart into a desert place and asked them the world's opinion of him. "Whom do men say that I, the Son of Man, am?" They answered that some thought he was the great prophet Jeremiah, and others were sure that he was one of the great prophets; but some thought that he was Elijah come back to earth. There was indeed much in the life of Elijah, both on his sterner side and on his gentler side, which suggests the life of Christ. On the gentler side we have that similarity to Christ brought out in the story of the widow of Zarephath. It was after Elijah had come from the Brook Cherith in the mountains whither he had fled from the wrath of King Ahab after pronouncing the judgment of the drought upon the land, and where he had been sustained by water out of the brook and by the meat which the ravens brought him every morning and every evening. But after a time the brook dried up, and Elijah was directed to go to the town of Zarephath in Sidon, where he would find a widow who would sustain him. Into that same region our Lord once went, and there he performed one of his most gracious miracles when he healed the only daughter of a poor widow.

When Elijah arrived at the town, he saw this woman gathering sticks to build a fire, and said to her, "Fetch me, I pray thee, a little water in the vessel, that I may drink." As she went off to get him the drink of water, Elijah called after her and said, "Bring me, I pray thee, a morsel of bread in thine hand." At that the woman threw up her hands in a gesture of despair, and exclaimed, "As the Lord thy God liveth, I have not a cake, but an handful of meal in a barrel, and a little oil in a cruse: and, behold, I am gathering two sticks, that I may go in and dress it for me and my son, that we may eat it, and die." But Elijah said to her, "Fear not. Make me thereof a little cake first, and bring it unto me, and afterward make for thee and for thy son. .... The barrel of meal shall not waste, neither shall the cruse of oil fail." And that was exactly what happened. And in all the ages since, that phrase, "The widow's barrel of meal and the widow's cruse of oil," has stood for the providence of God and his care in our lives. Elijah is here. Underneath and about us are the everlasting arms. Therefore, be of good courage.

II

THE JUDGMENTS OF GOD AND DIVINE RETRIBUTION

When we say, Elijah is here, it means also the judgments of God, that there is a law, inexorable and inescapable, of divine justice and retribution at work in the world. The whole career of Elijah and the judgments which he pronounced upon the wicked court and the apostate nation reveal this important and impressive truth, that God's eyes are on the wicked, and that though hand join in hand, they shall not go unpunished.

True religion and morality had almost disappeared in the land of Israel. Under the domination of his wicked and idolatrous wife, Jezebel, Ahab had sunk the nation in sin. The bull god Baal was set up all over the land, and the worshipers of Jehovah were proscribed and persecuted. It was in view of that fact that God sent Elijah to pronounce his judgments. The announcement of Obadiah to Ahab, "Elijah is here," was equivalent to saying, "Elijah is here; therefore, you and your false prophets of Baal had better tremble."

In view of what is going on in the world today, it is a mighty reinforcement to our faith and courage to remember that Elijah is here; that is, that God has not forsaken the world, that he has not forsaken his people, that he beholds the injustice and the iniquity which are done on the earth. God keeps books; and although he does not pay at the end of every week, nevertheless he pays.

Not only did the presence of Elijah mean a judgment upon the whole nation, but also upon Ahab in particular for an act of great wickedness and cruelty. One evening, taking the air, Ahab came upon a vineyard, of which the location and the cultivated fruitful state, with its well-kept tower and fruitful vines, struck him as making a property greatly to be desired—all the more so because it was near his palace in Jezreel. Ahab inquired of some of his officers as to who the owner was, and when he learned that it was Naboth, he sent him a proposal, offering a sum of money for the vineyard;

or, if he preferred, he would buy him another vineyard even better than it. But to his astonishment Naboth declined the offer. The king probably offered him twice as much the second time, but still Naboth refused to sell. It had been in his family, he said, for generations, and he would not part with it for any sum of money. It is always refreshing to find a man like that, whether he lives in the days of Elijah, or in the twentieth century. Neither Naboth nor his vineyard was for sale.

That night the disappointed Ahab came to his palace heavy and displeased, and like a spoiled child would not sit down to his dinner, but lay down on his bed and turned his face to the wall. The queen, Jezebel, the real man around that palace, and the Lady Macbeth of the Old Testament, came in to the king and asked him, "What is the trouble? Why are you lying there on the bed with that dismal expression on your face? Why don't you get up and eat your dinner?" Ahab then related to her the incident of the vineyard, and how Naboth refused to sell it. When she heard the story, Jezebel said, "What kind of a king are you anyway? Get up and eat your dinner, and be merry in heart, and leave Naboth's vineyard to me." Then the wicked queen wrote letters to her officers and sealed them with the seal of Ahab. In the letters she gave directions to the officers in the city to have Naboth arrested and charged with blasphemy by false witnesses. This was done. The innocent, high-minded, and courageous Naboth was brought to trial and convicted of blasphemy against God. The punishment was death by stoning. The stoning took place just near the pool of Samaria where the harlots bathed. After Naboth had been stoned to death, the scavenger dogs gathered round and greedily licked up the blood that flowed from his mangled body.

Then word was sent to Jezebel that Naboth was dead, and Jezebel told the king to go down and possess the vineyard, "for," she said, "Naboth is not alive, but dead." Yes, Naboth was dead; but God was not dead, and retribution was not dead, and Elijah was not dead. The king, in great delight, went down to possess the vineyard; but he had hardly entered the gates of the vineyard, and had not yet tasted of the first of its ripe grapes, when he was confronted by none other than Elijah. Behold, Elijah is here! When Ahab saw the prophet of God, he exclaimed, "Hast thou found me, O mine enemy?" Elijah answered, "I have found thee." Elijah was conscience! Conscience cannot be stoned to death. Conscience cannot be bribed. Conscience cannot be killed. To every doer of evil it will say, eventually, "I have found thee."

Elijah, standing before the guilty king, prophesied Ahab's death, and also this incident in connection

ELIJAH—THE SON OF THUNDER

with his death: "Where dogs licked the blood of Naboth shall dogs lick thy blood, even thine." After that Ahab had no delight in the vineyard. Whenever he went out to walk of an evening, he was sure to pass it by, for he could hear the blood of Naboth calling from the earth for vengeance; and wherever he went there followed him the awful echo of Elijah's words, "Where dogs licked the blood of Naboth shall dogs lick thy blood, even thine."

But the weeks and the months and the years passed by and nothing happened. Ahab no doubt thought that the judgment pronounced upon him by Elijah had missed fire. But one day he went up to battle with Jehoshaphat, the king of Judah, against the Syrian stronghold, Ramoth-Gilead. As the chariots were rolling to and fro, and the armies were maneuvering for the onset of the battle, Ahab remembered Elijah's melancholy prediction, and taking off his royal robes, disguised himself as a private soldier. Thus he hoped to escape vengeance and death in the battle. But a certain man, one of those anointed agents of divine retribution, drew his mighty bow at a venture, not aiming at any one in particular. But the arrow was aimed by the hand of God. It smote Ahab in the joints of his harness and inflicted a mortal wound. The king courageously stayed himself up in the chariot until the sun was set, when he died. Then, in the retreat of his army his chariot with his dead body in it was driven back to Jezreel. The charioteer drove the bloody chariot down to the pool of Samaria to wash out the blood that had flowed from the king's wounds; and as he did so, the dogs, the very dogs that there had licked the blood of Naboth, gathered round and licked up the blood of Ahab from the floor of his chariot.

Elijah is here! Let evildoers and tyrants tremble. Czechoslovakia is crushed. Poland is a shambles and a waste. Heroic Finland, worthy to take its place with the three hundred Spartans who fell at Thermopylae, has had to yield to the brutal Antichrist of Russia. Greece is fallen. Nevertheless, let the tyrants and dictators beware. Elijah is here! God has not abdicated his throne. There is a law of retribution and of justice which works among men and nations and which will not fail of its vengeance.

III

THE POWER OF PRAYER

When we say, Elijah is here, it means that we have the power and the help of prayer. In his reference to Elijah, James adds to our knowledge of Elijah and the great judgment of the drought that fell upon the land. In the story in the Book of Kings we are told merely that Elijah predicted the drought, but James says that this judgment came in answer to the prayer of Elijah. James says: "Elias was a man subject to like passions as we are, and he prayed earnestly that it might not rain: and it rained not on the earth by the space of three years and six months. And he prayed again, and the heaven gave rain, and the earth brought forth her fruit." James says this in connection with his statement that "the effectual fervent prayer of a righteous man availeth much."

All the great events in the life of Elijah show the power of prayer and how effectual the prayer of a godly man is. He prayed that it might not rain, and it rained not on the earth for the space of three years and a half. He prayed again, and there was rain on the earth. Dramatic, too, is the story of how Elijah relied upon prayer in his battle with the priests of Baal. He had challenged them and the whole nation to the trial by fire. After the priests of Baal had leaped and danced and cut themselves with stone and prayed in vain to Baal to send down fire and consume the offerings, Elijah built his altar and drenched the offering with water, and then offered his heartfelt prayer: "Hear me, O Lord, hear me, that this people may know that thou art the Lord God, and that thou hast turned their heart back again." When he had so prayed the fire fell from heaven and consumed the burnt offering and the water that filled the trenches.

Then Elijah announced to Ahab that the rain was coming. He sent his servant to the top of Carmel while he himself cast himself on the ground, and with his head between his knees called upon God. The servant stood on the top of Carmel, and looking off over the Mediterranean, saw not a sign of rain. The sky was like brass, the sea like glass without a ruffle on its surface. When he went back to his master Elijah he said, "There is nothing." Elijah told him to go and look again, and again he went to the top of Carmel, while Elijah lay on the ground with his head between his knees. Again the young man returned to Elijah and said, "There is nothing," and the prophet told him to go again. He went again the third time, and the fourth time, and the fifth time, and the sixth time, and every time he reported, "There is nothing." But Elijah told him to go the seventh time; and this time when he looked, behold, a cloud on the horizon no larger than a man's hand. Soon there was the rush of the wind and the sound of the abundance of rain, and Elijah girding up his loins ran in triumph before Ahab to his palace at Jezreel. Behold, Elijah is here. When you pray, remember Elijah.

ELIJAH—THE SON OF THUNDER

IV

THE CERTAINTY AND THE GLORY OF THE LIFE TO COME

When we say, "Elijah is here," it means that we live after death and that that life is one of power and glory. There was a grandeur, and a pathos, too, about the translation of Elijah and the end of his earthly life. A lonely man all his days, Elijah wanted to be alone when the end came. But the faithful Elisha would not leave him. Together, therefore, they went down to the Jordan, where Elijah took his mantle and smote the waters, and together they went over the river. Then as they talked together, behold, a chariot of fire and horses of fire parted them asunder and Elijah went up in a whirlwind into heaven.

That sublime ending to Elijah's earthly life was in itself a magnificent testimony to the truth that good men never die, that death cannot conquer them, that they have their high and exceeding great reward. But in the history of Elijah as it is completed by the inspired penman of the New Testament, we have something even greater than that sublime scene by the Jordan when Elijah went up to heaven in a whirlwind.

With Peter and James and John, Jesus climbed

to the top of the mountain; and there, while the disciples slept, and as he prayed, Jesus was transfigured before them, and his countenance was bright with the glory of heaven. When the disciples awoke, to their amazement they saw Moses and Elijah standing by the side of Jesus and conversing with him. How exciting must have been their exclamation as Peter said to James, and James said to John, "Behold, Elijah is here!"

The appearance of Elijah in glory by the side of our Lord on the Mount of Transfiguration declares the fact of the glory of our life after death. Elijah is not a great memory merely; he is not the citizen of a sepulcher, he is not a handful of dust blown about the Syrian hills, but a living man, a living soul, for God is not the God of the dead, but of the living. Elijah, with all the power of his mind, appears in the fellowship of Moses and of Christ and converses with them about the great fact of all the ages.

And what was that fact? What was the theme and subject of Elijah and Moses when they talked to Christ? It was that subject upon which God himself first spoke when he said to the man and the woman after the fall that the seed of the woman should bruise the head of the serpent. It was the fact of which God spoke to Abraham when he told him to offer up Isaac on Mount Moriah, and told him that because of his obedience in him all nations of the earth should be blessed. It was the subject of which Balaam sang when he said, "There shall come a star out of Jacob, and a sceptre shall rise out of Israel." It was the subject of which God spake to Moses when he gave him instruction for the altars of sacrifice and the Day of Atonement; the subject of which David sang when he spoke of Christ and his kingdom; the subject of which Jeremiah spoke when he said the day would come when God would make a New Covenant with his people; the subject of which Isaiah spoke when he painted his great picture of the One who was despised and rejected of men, the Man of Sorrows and acquainted with grief; the subject of which Peter spoke when he said that we have been redeemed not with corruptible things, but with the precious blood of Christ, as a lamb without spot and blemish; the subject in which Paul gloried when he said, "God forbid that I should glory, save in the cross of our Lord Jesus Christ"; the subject which John on his Isle of exile said was the great Theme, and the great Music of the New Jerusalem, when he saw the multitude that had come out of great tribulation and washed their robes and made them white in the blood of the Lamb. And what subject is this? It is the power of God unto salvation, the power of the Cross to save from sin. That was what Elijah and Moses talked to

Christ about; the majesty of it, the sublimity of it, the ineffable glory of it!

Elijah is here! And he will be here as long as the Cross of Christ is here. Compared with that great fact, what else is worth speaking of? I can imagine that when we get to heaven and are surrounded by all its indescribable splendors and beauties, and are permitted to associate with all its illustrious citizens, we shall say to one another, "Behold, Samuel is here"; "Behold, David is here"; "Behold, Isaiah is here"; "Behold, Jeremiah is here"; "Behold, Hosea is here"; "Behold, John the Baptist is here"; "Behold, Peter is here"; "Behold, John is here"; "Behold, Paul is here." And after we have run to meet them and greet them and to hear them, then I think I shall hear someone say, "Behold, Elijah is here." And at that we shall go to seek out Elijah, and finding him again in the company of Moses, we shall say to him—as we call to all our friends, "Elijah is here"—we shall say to him, "Elijah, tell us now what you and Moses said to one another and to Christ when you talked with him about his death on the Cross."

The angels can say to God, "Behold, Elijah is here!" Through your faith in Christ, through your fidelity to God, will the angels of heaven be able to say to God, substituting your name for the name of Elijah, "Behold, he is here"?

X

SAMUEL—THE MAN WHO PREACHED FROM THE GRAVE

"Bring me up Samuel."

I SAMUEL 28:11

No WITCH SCENE FROM SHAKESPEARE OR THE writers of fiction can surpass in awe and gripping interest this scene at the Cave of Endor, where the woman with the familiar spirit bends over her cauldron. Saul had been a great soldier; but now the time had come for Saul to fight his last battle. Haggard and haunted with care, Saul leaned on his sword on Mount Gilboa and surveyed the host of the Philistines who lay beneath him all along the valley, that most fought over soil on this planet, the Valley of Esdraelon.

From where he stood Saul could see the lights of the campfires of the Philistine army. He heard the hum of that host, the shouts of the captains, the neighing of the horses, the blare of the trumpets.

In this crisis Saul felt the need of a higher power than his own right arm and reached out after the help of the unseen. "Saul inquired of the Lord." In his brief reign he had too often neglected to do that, and had followed his own way; but at last he sought after the help of God. There was no prophet to whom he could go for Samuel was dead. What would Saul not have given now for the presence and the counsel of Samuel? Then he tried to get a sign from the Urim and the Thummim, perhaps the mystic stones which flashed and gleamed upon the breastplate of the high priest. But no guiding ray came from them. For one who would learn the secrets of tomorrow there was only one course left, and that was to consult a necromancer, one who dealt in the secrets of the occult world. In his despair Saul asked his servants to let him know if there was a woman with a familiar spirit who was available. To consult such a person was contrary to the law of God and was outlawed by Saul himself, upon penalty of death. Now Saul proceeded to break his own law.

His kingly robes and armor have been laid aside, and in disguise Saul and his attendants make their way to the cave of the Witch of Endor, not more than six miles from Nazareth, where Jesus was brought up. Even in his disguise, it was strange that the witch did not know him, for Saul towered head and shoulders over all Israel. Indeed, we rather gather from the narrative that the witch did recognize him, because when Saul appeared at her den and asked her to bring up whomsoever he should name, the woman reminded him of the decree of Saul and besought him not to lay a snare for her life. Being reassured by Saul that he would protect her from all harm and punishment, the woman said to the king, "Whom shall I bring up?"

For whom did Saul ask? Whom now in his hour of great need and great anxiety would he have brought up out of the unseen world? Perhaps Abraham, who was the friend of God? Or Moses, with whom God spoke face to face? Or Joshua, the greatest soldier and captain of them all? Or Gideon who had smitten the host of the Midianites? But no; it was for none of these that Saul asked. This was his request, and there was never a more earnest, or sincere, or beautiful, or moving, or pathetic request, although uttered here in a witch's den. "Bring me up Samuel!" Bring up Samuel! He is the one to whom I would talk, Samuel, the prophet of the Lord; Samuel who anointed me as king and kissed me; Samuel who gave me another spirt and turned me into another man; Samuel who so earnestly warned me and rebuked me, when I had disobeyed the Lord, and prayed over me, and wept over me. If anyone can help me now, if anyone can foretell my fate in the battle tomorrow with the Philistine host, it is Samuel. Bring me up Samuel!

God, not the witch, answered Saul's prayer. When the frightened fakir, the woman with the familiar spirit, saw that Samuel was actually coming out of

Sheol, she fell on her face in terror. Apparently Samuel was not yet visible to Saul, for he asked the woman what she saw. She said, "I see gods ascending out of the earth." "What form is he of?" asked Saul. The woman replied, "An old man is cometh up; and he is covered with a mantle." At this Saul perceived that this was Samuel and bowed his face to the ground in reverence and obeisance.

But Saul, alas! had turned to Samuel too late, for Samuel said to Saul, "Why hast thou disquieted me to bring me up?" Saul answered, "I am sore distressed; for the Philistines make war against me, and God is departed from me, and answereth me no more, neither by prophet, nor by dreams; therefore have I called thee, that thou mayest make known unto me what I shall do."

Then answered the shade of Samuel: "Wherefore then dost thou ask of me, seeing the Lord is departed from thee, and is become thine enemy? . . . . The Lord will deliver also Israel with thee into the hand of the Philistines: and tomorrow shalt thou and thy sons be with me." With that the soul of Samuel vanished again.

This is the only sermon in the Bible that was ever preached by a preacher who had come from the grave. The rich man in hell asked that Lazarus should be sent from the dead to preach to his five wicked brothers, but that request was not granted.

SAMUEL—WHO PREACHED FROM THE GRAVE

Here is the only preacher who ever went unto men from the dead. Here is the only sermon that was ever preached by a man who had passed into the world of the dead. And what a sermon it is! It proclaims with a voice more eloquent even than that of Isaiah and Paul, who are the authors of that searching and arresting saying, "Now is the accepted time, and now is the day of salvation."

Samuel is the man who preaches from his grave; and today, not out of a witch's cauldron, nor by the waving wand or incantation of a woman with a familiar spirit, but by the inspired page of the Old Testament, we would call up Samuel and have him preach to us.

I

SAMUEL AND A GODLY MOTHER

The first thing that Samuel tells us is the power of the prayer of a godly mother. Samuel was born in answer to the earnest, fervent prayer of a godly woman. She prayed so earnestly there in the Holy House at Shiloh that the aging priest, dozing on his priestly seat, seeing her lips move, but hearing no word, denounced her for a drunken woman and bade her leave the sacred precincts. But Hannah explained to him that it was out of the abundance of her grief that she had prayed. When her prayer was answered and the child was born, she called him

Samuel, "Because I have asked him of the Lord." Hannah never forgot that fact that she had asked this child of the Lord, and for that reason she dedicated him to the Lord. She took him up to the Sacred House and said to the priest, "As long as he liveth, he shall be lent to the Lord."

It is not by accident that in the Bible we are informed in so many instances as to the character of the great man's ancestors. We know what kind of father and mother John the Baptist had, how they were both righteous in the sight of the Lord. We hear of the prayers and the faith unfeigned of Timothy's mother and grandmother; of the God-fearing devotion of the mother of Moses; of how Manoah and his wife asked the angel how they should train their child Samson. Men do not gather grapes of thorns nor figs of thistles, and almost always back of the strong man is a strong praying mother.

Lincoln often thought of that mother who, when she was dying, called him and his sister into the rude cabin at Gentryville, Indiana, and laying her hand upon his head, told him she was going on a long journey from which she would not return, and asked him to be kind to his sister, to obey his father, and to love God. Years afterwards, the great man said, "All I am, or ever hope to be, I owe to my angel mother." Grover Cleveland, one of our strongest presidents, a man who in early life wandered far from the right path, attributed his success to his mother's prayers, and kept hanging on his wall the framed motto that his mother had given him, "As thy days so shall thy strength be."

The celebrated Dr. McCosh of Princeton had the custom of calling in the members of the senior class one by one and having prayer with them before they left the college and went out into the university of experience and life. One young man surprised Dr. McCosh, and grieved him, by refusing to let him pray with him, saying he did not believe that there was a God and that prayer was altogether futile. Dr. McCosh then bade him farewell.

Some years later he was giving a series of lectures in Cincinnati. Sitting in the hotel lobby one night before going to the hall where he was to lecture, he was accosted by a stranger who sat down beside him and said to him, "What is this I hear, Dr. McCosh, about your turning out infidels at Princeton?" Surprised, Dr. McCosh asked him what he meant. Then he gave him the name of the young man who had refused to let him pray with him when he was leaving Princeton. The man told him that he was now at the head of one of the important high schools in the city and was exerting a most harmful influence upon the lives of the young people who passed under his instruction. "But," added the man, "he has a devout praying mother, and I believe that in the end his mother's prayers will win."

Some years later a man whom he did not recognize walked into Dr. McCosh's study at Princeton and introduced himself as the young man who, some years before, in that very room, had refused to let him pray for him. Through his mother's prayers, he said, a complete change had been wrought in him, and he had come to Princeton with his wife to enter the Theological Seminary and prepare himself for the Christian ministry. "Now, Dr. McCosh," he said, "will you kneel down with me and offer that long postponed prayer?"

Yes, who can estimate the power of a mother's prayers? What the church needs today is more women like Hannah, who are ready to lend their sons unto the Lord.

II

SAMUEL'S CALL

This is a fact worth pausing over, that in the case of nearly all the great men of God who appear in the Bible we hear of how they were called through some special particular experience and manifestation of the presence of God. It was so with Abraham in his vision of the night; with Gideon when he was given the sign of the fleece and the flame; with Moses who saw the bush burn yet not consumed;

with Isaiah who saw the glory of the Lord, high and lifted up, in the Temple; with Paul who saw the bright light from heaven and heard a voice saying, "Saul, Saul, why persecutest thou me?" Samuel is no exception to that rule. There he lies, a little lad sleeping in his bed in Shiloh's Holy House. That, above all places, is the best place to hear the voice of God. Take your child to Shiloh; take him to the church, and even when you least think it he may hear the voice of God speaking to his soul.

Ere the lamp of God had gone out in the Holy House, Samuel heard a voice speaking to him, "Samuel"; and rising he went over to the aged Eli, and said, "Here am I; for thou calledst me." But when Eli told him that he had not called him, the wondering boy went back to his bed and lay down again. A second time he heard the voice, and a second time Eli told him he had not called his name. But when Samuel came the third time the old priest perceived that God was speaking to the boy, and told him, "If you hear that voice again, saying, Samuel, then answer, Speak, Lord, for thy servant heareth." When for the fourth time Samuel heard the voice calling him, that was his answer, "Speak, Lord, for thy servant heareth." That henceforth is the motto of Samuel's great life. Whenever God speaks, Samuel listens and obeys.

God puts him at this first call to a severe test, for

he reveals to him the fearful judgment which is to befall Eli and his house and his family. No wonder, with sleep not again touching his eyelids, Samuel feared to tell the dread tidings to the priest. But he was faithful to the word of God and told Eli all that he had heard. "And Samuel told him every whit, and hid not a word from him." Israel needed that kind of a prophet and preacher then. The church needs him today. Always the request will be as in the days of Isaiah, "Prophesy unto us smooth sayings." But the gospel is not always smooth sayings. There are hard sayings also. There are sayings of judgment and warning and retribution. Even to the very last, there were hard things that Samuel had to say, and hardest of all that last sermon that he preached to his old friend, King Saul, "Tomorrow shalt thou and thy sons be with me."

III

SAMUEL IN THE HOUR OF ADVERSITY

The third thing Samuel preaches from the grave is how to carry ourselves in the hour of trial and adversity. Just as a coin which through much usage has grown so smooth that the date and the inscriptions on it cannot be read, when heated in the fire reveals the date and the inscription again, so adversity and trial bring out the real inscription on a man's

SAMUEL—WHO PREACHED FROM THE GRAVE

soul. What a wonderful inscription adversity revealed in the soul of Samuel!

After his illustrious career as the great leader and prophet of Israel, a delegation of the people waited on him one day and told him that the time had come for him to resign and step aside. "Behold, thou art old. .... Now make us a king." Nor did they hesitate in their cruelty to remind Samuel of the fact that his unworthy sons "walked not in the way of the Lord." That heavy cross, together with many another godly man, Samuel had to bear, the cross of unworthy, ungodly children.

In this difficult hour Samuel did nothing common or mean. He proceeded at the direction of the Lord to help them choose a king, and then when the king was established on his throne, he bade the people farewell in one of the noblest valedictories that ever fell from the lips of man. Like Paul in his beautiful valedictory to the elders of the church of Ephesus at Miletus, Samuel challenged them to question his integrity, or to point to a single dishonorable act in his long experience with them. Instead of rebuking them for their folly in rejecting him and choosing a king, Samuel reminded them of the mercies of God and that if they returned to God and repented, God would not forsake his people. "Only fear the Lord, and serve him in truth with all your heart."

Then came this beautiful farewell: "As for me,

God forbid that I should sin against the Lord in ceasing to pray for you." That was spoken by Samuel ages before Christ stood on the mount and said, "Love your enemies, and pray for them that despitefully use you." But here we find Samuel anticipating the teaching of our Lord. That, indeed, is the way to bear adversity; that, indeed, is the way to deal with those whom we think have hurt us or wounded us or injured us. Pray for them. That will take the sting out of the wound. "As for me, God forbid that I should cease to pray for you."

IV

SAMUEL AS THE HOLY SPIRIT TO THE SOUL OF SAUL

For the person and the work of the Holy Spirit, one of the best biblical illustrations and explanations is the relationship of Samuel to King Saul.

First of all, came the call of God's Spirit, and Saul's appointment. As the representative of God, Samuel went to Saul and told him of his high destiny. When Saul wondered at it, Samuel said, "And on whom is all the desire of Israel? Is it not on thee?" So God's Holy Spirit comes to us reminding us that we are made in God's image and that there is a glorious destiny in store for us if we will

SAMUEL—WHO PREACHED FROM THE GRAVE

submit ourselves to the divine influence and obey the divine voice.

Saul had a great possibility. All that was desirable in Israel could have been his. But how sad is that sentence which tells us of the end of Saul, when he fell there on Mount Gilboa, "Saul took a sword and fell on it." Alas! where are all the children born in Christian homes, presented to God in the waters of baptism, reared in the church, anointed with prayer as Saul was anointed with oil? How many of them have failed and come short of their great destiny, like Saul's, their bow and their shield vilely cast away as if they had not been anointed with oil. The Spirit of God came mightily upon Saul and turned him for a little into another man. But Saul resisted that Spirit, and the greatest shipwreck in the Bible was the consequence.

Next we see Samuel, who had called and anointed Saul, pleading and warning him. So the Holy Spirit which calls us to God pleads with us and warns us when we turn away from him. Again and again Samuel went to Saul, and again and again Saul said, "I have sinned," only to turn again to a new transgression, till Samuel cried all night over Saul to God. What a picture that is of God's Holy Spirit pleading with the soul to do his will, and saying to us as God said of old to His people, "How can I let thee go?"

At length there comes the final break in the relationship of Samuel and Saul. It is related in what seems to me one of the saddest sentences of the Bible: "And Samuel came no more to see Saul until the day of his death." No more of those visits, no more of those pleadings, no more of those warnings, no more of those tears. "Samuel came no more to see Saul." Saul has sinned away his day of grace. What that "no more" means Saul will learn on the day of his death.

Samuel was a man who lived in Israel ages ago; but still this history of Samuel and Saul speaks to every heart. God calls you, God appoints you to a noble destiny, to what Paul called immortality and glory. For you too is all that is desirable in life and destiny. Are you, like Saul, resisting God's Holy Spirit? Is there any habit of your life against which the Spirit is warning you? Is there any course in your life which the Spirit is showing you to be wrong? Is there any decision that the Spirit has told you you must make, and yet you defer it? Then learn from Saul, who drove Samuel from him. "Samuel came no more to see Saul until the day of his death."

This mighty Samuel who emerges from the shades of Sheol preaches many great sermons to us. He preaches of the power of a mother's prayer. He preaches of the possible greatness of every human

SAMUEL—WHO PREACHED FROM THE GRAVE

life, of fortitude and forgiveness in the hour of trial. But the most earnest and solemn word that this preacher from the grave has to say is that life and opportunity come to their end. Belief and repentance are for today, and then cometh tomorrow when we shall be with both Samuel and Saul in the land where there is no repentance. Then heed his voice, "Seek ye the Lord while he may be found, call ye upon him while he is near: resist not his Holy Spirit, for the night cometh." How shall the night find you? As it found Saul, resisting God's Holy Spirit? Or as it found Samuel, the servant of God, doing the will of God even in the hour of death?

XI

JOHN THE BAPTIST—THE FRIEND OF THE BRIDEGROOM[1]

> "Among them that are born of women there hath not risen a greater than John the Baptist."
>
> MATTHEW 11:11

ONCE ON A BRIGHT JUNE DAY I STOOD UPON A summit of the Blue Ridge Mountains. To the north and to the south stretched the mountains, their mighty shoulders draped with a haze of infinite blue. In front of me lay the Cumberland Valley, well watered, like the Garden of the Lord. I could see the fields and orchards with their alternate hues like checkered squares; the white ribbons which marked the fine highways along which half a century ago might have been seen the eager soldiery of Lee as his army marched into Pennsylvania; the enormous red barns, the white towers of the hamlet churches, the gray stone farmhouses, and man going forth to his labor until the evening. I had often passed through that valley, but it was only when I stood upon the summit of the mountain that I was able to see it in all its length and breadth.

---

[1] Reprinted from *Of Them He Chose Twelve,* by Clarence E. Macartney, by permission of Dorrance and Company, publishers.

JOHN THE BAPTIST—FRIEND OF BRIDEGROOM

There are times when it is good for us to get above the smoke and dust and confusion of our everyday existence and look at life from some great eminence, where the winds blow fresh and clear and the view is unobstructed. And what better place to stand than upon the shoulders of one of God's great men?

In his life of Thomas Carlyle, John Nicholl quotes a saying of Hegel that "a great man condemns the world to the task of explaining him." In the case of John the Baptist such condemnation is neither unpleasant nor unprofitable. John's brief and fiery ministry of judgment and repentance had come to a close. Because of his fearless denunciation of Herod and Herodias for their adulterous union, John had been cast into prison. There in the lonely dungeon of Machaerus, on the shore of the Dead Sea, John's mighty spirit began to flag and his eagle eye began to film with doubt. "Art thou he that should come, or do we look for another?" That was the question John sent to Jesus from the dungeon. The answer of Christ was marked by that deep respect with which he always referred to his great forerunner: "Go and shew John again those things which ye do hear and see: the blind receive their sight, and the lame walk, the lepers are cleansed, and the deaf hear, the dead are raised up, and the poor have the gospel preached to them. And blessed is he, whosoever shall not be offended in me." That was for John. This world flatters a man to his face and disparages him when his back is turned. Not so Christ. He did not tell John that he was the greatest man that ever lived; but when the messengers of John had gone their way, Jesus turned to the crowd who stood about and who had overheard the conversation, and perhaps now doubted that John was a prophet, and said to them: "What went ye out into the wilderness to see? A reed shaken with the wind?" A man answering every wind of popular opinion like one of the reeds in the Jordan Valley, bending before the vagrant wind? "A man clothed in soft raiment," or looking for a soft place? "But what went ye out for to see? A prophet? Yea, I say unto you, and more than a prophet. . . . . Verily I say unto you, Among them that are born of women there hath not arisen a greater than John the Baptist." If praise is to be measured by the lips which pronounce it, then never was man so praised as was John the Baptist. In speaking, then, about the greatness of John we shall think, first, of the origin of his greatness, whence it came, and, second, of the content of his greatness—what it was.

Let us trace this great river back to its source. The other John, writing of the Baptist, said, "There was a man sent from God, whose name was John." That was as far as John could go in accounting for

JOHN THE BAPTIST—FRIEND OF BRIDEGROOM

the greatness of the Baptist. It is as far as any man can go, for over the unfathomed depths of great personality there broods a mystery like that which hovers over the face of the sleeping ocean. Back of all our histories and biographies and heredity and environment and education lies the mighty purpose of God. When the world needs its great soul, God has him in reserve, and there is a man sent from God.

But in sending such men into the world, God lets them come through channels and instrumentalities which lie within our observation. I was reading, some time ago, the life of a distinguished American soldier, Albert Sidney Johnston. He and his family had lived for generations in Virginia, but this story of his life did not commence in Virginia. It commenced away across the seas, beneath a thatch-roofed cottage on the shores of the Solway Firth in Scotland. All true biography commences with genealogy. If John was the greatest man that ever lived, this is the first thing we want to know about him. Who was his father? Who was his mother? Of what race and stock did he come? What were the streams which contributed to the river of this great life? Luke, who is always the explicit and careful historian, lays great stress on this fact. He says there was a "certain priest named Zacharias, ... and his wife of the daughters of Aaron, and her name was Elisabeth; and they were both righteous before God."

In a letter in which he stated his qualifications for a position as tutor for which he was applying, Carlyle wrote: "Not forgetting among my other advantages the prayers of religious parents, a blessing which, if I speak less of it, I do not feel less than he." It is a blessed thing to have had a godly father, whose example is still with you, and a blessed thing to have had a pious mother, whose prayers and whose love still attend you. But it is still a more blessed thing, a still greater responsibility, to have had a father and mother who were both "righteous before God," and into whose dear, pure, calm, overcoming faces you can look in any hour of danger when life would frighten you with its tragedy, or when temptation would lure you from the path of truth and duty, whose voices call to you even from their graves and bid you hold fast to God and do the right at every cost.

Born of such parents, from the day that he was able to think, John was taught to deny himself; "He shall be great in the sight of the Lord, and shall drink neither wine nor strong drink; and he shall be filled with the Holy Ghost, even from his mother's womb." John's rude garments of skins and camel hair and his diet of locusts and wild honey did not make him great, but it is worth noting that luxury and self-indulgence had no place in the training of the man whom Christ was to call the greatest

JOHN THE BAPTIST—FRIEND OF BRIDEGROOM

of the sons of men. He whose preaching is to condemn the world must himself have given no pledges to the world. We frequently speak of a good environment for our children and our young people, and by it we generally mean "all the opportunities which money can buy, little responsibility, and none of the self-discipline which reveals the hidden powers and which alone should be counted a good environment."

After his training in that home of piety and self-denial, John was trained in the desert. He "was in the deserts till the day of his shewing unto Israel." John's character was shaped in solitude. He retired from the face of man that he might see more clearly the face of God. "No man," said Thomas De Quincey, "will ever unfold the capacities of his intellect who does not at least checker his life with solitude." In the solitude of the desert, in the midst of a great physical loneliness, John learned to meet and endure that moral loneliness which men fear above all else and yet which must so often be the lot of God's true servants. Think of this greatest of all preachers and prophets, with only the Dead Sea and the undulating desert for his seminary, and with the ruins of Sodom and Gomorrah for his illuminated text, waiting until the thought of God, the grandest thought which can take possession of mortal man, took hold of him:

THE GREATEST MEN OF THE BIBLE

"I think he had not heard of the far towns,
Nor of the dreams of men, nor of king's crowns,
   Until the thought of God took hold of him
And he was sitting dreaming in the calm
   Of the first noon upon the desert's rim."[2]

We have seen the source of John's greatness. Now what was that greatness? How did it express itself?

I

THE GREATNESS OF CONVICTION

There has never been a great life, a great witness, without a great conviction back of it. John was no agnostic, telling the world what he was not sure of, or what he could not believe; but with terrible earnestness he told the world what he did believe. It is the lack of conviction that threatens to kill preaching in the Protestant pulpit. What we need is not more knowledge, organization, paraphernalia, but more bedrock conviction as to a few great facts. John had a few tremendous convictions—that the Kingdom of God was at hand, that men must repent of their sins, that the Christ was at hand, and, when he saw him, that Jesus was the Christ. With these convictions he shook the world.

That deep conviction made John sincere and earnest in his preaching. He was a burning and a

---
[2] Edward Fitzgerald.

JOHN THE BAPTIST—FRIEND OF BRIDEGROOM

shining light. The light shone because it burned. Nothing can ever take the place of that sincerity which is born of conviction. We can respect sincere men however much we differ with them, but the most gifted of men forfeits our respect if he does not ring true. What is the difference, for instance, between two men like John the Baptist and Francis Bacon? Both were sons of genius. What would a man not give to have written the essay on Truth—"What is truth, said jesting Pilate, and would not stay for an answer"—or the essay on Death—"Men dread death as children fear to go in the dark!" Yet between those two men there yawns the gulf which stretches between sincerity and insincerity. "He chose," writes Bacon's biographer of him, "to please men and not to follow what his soul must have told him was the better way. He wanted in his dealings with men that sincerity upon which he so strongly insisted in his dealings with nature, and the ruin of a great life was the consequence."

II

THE GREATNESS OF HUMILITY

When John's disciples, jealous of the growing fame of Jesus, went to him in alarm and said, "Rabbi, ... the same baptizeth, and all men come to him," instead of fanning their discontent, John gave them his great answer: "The friend of the bridegroom, which standeth and heareth him, rejoiceth greatly because of the bridegroom's voice; .... He must increase, but I must decrease." It is not pleasant to be told that someone can write or sing or preach or administer better than we can. We would just as soon be told something else.

John never turned his own immense popularity to a selfish purpose. When his preaching was creating such a sensation, the priests and Levites sent a deputation out to interview him. They said to him, "Art thou the Christ?" "No." "Art thou Elijah?" "No." "Art thou one of the prophets? If not, who art thou? What shall we say to them that sent us? What explanation shall we give of these extraordinary scenes?" John might have claimed any of these titles, and the multitude would have gone with him. He could have founded a new religion or set up a new government. But the friend of the bridegroom was true to the bridegroom: "Tell your masters I am only a voice crying in the wilderness. Who I am makes no difference." When Wendell Phillips stood by the open grave of John Brown on the mountain top in the Adirondacks, he said, "How some men struggle into oblivion and others forget themselves into immortality!" Most men think too much of "who" and not enough of "what." Not far from Winchester in the Shenandoah Valley, that

JOHN THE BAPTIST—FRIEND OF BRIDEGROOM

starlit abbey of the Confederacy, there is a monument to Virginia's unknown dead. It bears this inscription: "Who they were none knows—what they were all know."

III

THE GREATNESS OF COURAGE

The world does not commonly associate humility and courage. It likes to listen to the man who gives himself out to be somewhat, and it discounts the humble man. Yet how often, when it comes to taking a stand for principle, and enduring the taunts and ridicule of the people, it is the meek and unassuming man who surprises us with the greatness of his courage. In some pathway through a deep glen of the forest you have come upon a jutting rock, covered with green moss, and through it there trickles a tiny cascade. Nothing on earth is softer than that moss, but when you tear away the moss you come upon the cold, naked rock. So underneath John's humility was the cold, naked, adamantine rock of incorruptible and indomitable courage. Let us see how he used that courage. The multitude flocked out to hear him and to see him, the crowds whose warm flattery has ruined so many preachers and prophets. But to them John said, "Repent! for the kingdom of heaven is at hand." Then came the publicans, the clever politicians and manipulators of the day: "Exact no more than that which is appointed you." And after the publicans came the soldiers, the men who could overturn the government of a province in a day, no doubt attracted by this great voice and saying to themselves, "With John for our leader what could we not do, what could we not conquer!" "Master, what shall we do?" And like the ring of one of their own short swords upon the helmet of a foe came back the answer: "Do violence to no man, neither accuse any falsely; and be content with your wages."

Last of all in this strange procession to the Jordan came the Pharisees and the Sadducees, an odd alliance—the Pharisees, who by the minutiae of their literality had almost choked the wells of Old Testament inspiration, and the proud Sadducees, rationalists and materialists, the modernists of their day, who disbelieved in angel and in spirit and looked with pity upon the ignorant rabble who could receive such a doctrine as the resurrection of the body. Yet these classes came to John, John of all men, and said, "Master, what shall we do?" That was John's great test. Did he truckle to them? Did he say, "I speak in my rough, denunciatory way to the common people, but with you, of course, it is a different matter. You represent the thinking and educated classes, and even if truth must be silenced or surrendered I must hold your favor and your patronage?" Was that the way John talked to these men? No, not that, but this: "Who hath warned you to flee from the wrath to come? Bring forth therefore fruits meet for repentance."

But there is one thing yet braver in John's preaching. It takes little courage to stand upon a platform and denounce at long range the sins of what we call "high society." It took real courage to do what John did. He marched into the palace itself and there, in the presence of the adulterous pair, said to Herod, "It is not lawful for thee to have her; you are breaking God's commandment and God will judge you." That sermon cost John his life. Oh, if John had been mobbed by the people, assassinated by the soldiers, or torn by a wild beast in the midst of one of his desert reveries, that, we think, had been a death in keeping with his life. But to think that he had to die at the whispered wish of a vindictive adulteress! The greatest man that ever lived, and here is his head on a silver charger to please the whim of a half-naked dancing girl! And the sun still smiles, the earth does not yawn to swallow up the authors of this infamy! But wait! The evangelist tells us that when John was dead his disciples came and took up the body and buried it, and went and told Jesus. John had friends, disciples, and I have no doubt that they wrapped his body in as clean a linen cloth as that which enwound the body of the Lord, and women anointed him with their tears. Perhaps in Jerusalem they buried the body, perhaps by Jordan's flood, and rolled a great stone to the door of the sepulcher and departed. "It" not "him," the body, not John! They could not bury John. Time has not been able to bury him; the ages have not been able to engulf him. No wonder guilty Herod, when he heard of the preaching of Jesus, stricken in conscience, cried out in fear and remorse, "John whom I beheaded is risen from the dead!" The soul of John the Baptist marches on; still cries his voice in the wilderness—every word that he uttered a battle, and his name like an army with banners!

IV

THE GREATNESS OF HIS MESSAGE

Shortly before his passion, Jesus went back to the Jordan country where he had been baptized by John and by the Holy Spirit. The disciples of John, now dead, gathered about Jesus and listened to him and saw his miracles. This was their verdict: "John did no miracle"—he never stilled the tempest, nor opened blind eyes, nor raised the dead—but all things that John spake of this man were true." What was it that John said about Jesus? Did he say, "Behold the man who did no sin and whose blameless life will leave the world a great example of how to live"? Did he say, "Behold the man, the carpenter's son who never wrote a line save in the dust, and yet the man whose words will do more to temper and soften and regenerate mankind than all the sayings of the philosophers and all the books of the sages"? Did he say, "Behold the man whose birth will be the watershed of history, dividing it into two parts, before Christ and after Christ"? Did he say, "Behold the man whose life shall be a fountain of compassion whence shall flow the healing streams of mercy and pity"? Did he say, "Behold the man who was in the world and yet not of it and who more than any other has brought life and immortality to life"? Did he say, "Behold the man whose death on the cross will be the supreme example of that vicarious suffering which runs like a scarlet thread through all creation"? Was that what John said of Jesus? If so, oblivion's sea had long ago swept over him. No, not that, but this—this which takes all that in, this which left out, Christianity is left out: "Behold the Lamb of God, which taketh away the sin of the world!"

It is that witness of John to Jesus that men today are trying to muffle and silence. The world will let you talk about Jesus as beautifully as you please. It will let you heap high the flowers of your eulogia; but there is one thing that the world cannot tolerate, and this is that you should say of Jesus what John said, "Behold the Lamb of God, which taketh away the sin of the world," God's eternal sacrifice for sin. Utter these words, and you will find that the Cross hath still its ancient offense. Leave them out, and you will find that then has the offense of the Cross ceased. This is the question before the church today: Shall the offense of the Cross cease? Shall the gospel cease to be good news and become only good advice? Shall the churches which have been entrusted with the gospel become lighthouses whose light has been quenched, or still worse, lighthouses which burn and flash with false lights which allure to destruction voyagers on the sea of life?

"Behold the Lamb of God, which taketh away the sin of the world!" Wherever that is left out, Christianity is left out. Wherever it is spoken and honored, there the gospel is preached, whether from the incense-laden altars of Greek and Roman Catholic Churches or in the severe dignity of our Reformed Churches, or in a gospel mission, or to the accompaniment of a bass drum on the street, or when at eventide a mother tells her little child of the love of God in Christ. Man is still a sinner, and still his great need is redemption from sin. Calvary has no successor; the Lamb of God has no substitute. He is the sinner's only hope. He is the power and glory of the church here; and hereafter it is the Lamb of

God, no longer upon the Cross but upon the throne of the universe, to whom redeemed sinners will pay their grateful homage.

"And I beheld and heard the voice of many angels round about the throne . . . . and the number of them was ten thousand times ten thousand, and thousands of thousands; saying with a loud voice, Worthy is the Lamb that was slain to receive power, and riches, and wisdom, and strength, and honor, and glory, and blessing. And every creature which is in heaven, and on the earth, and under the earth, and such as are in the sea, and all things that are in them, heard I saying, Blessing, and honor, and glory, and power, be unto him that sitteth upon the throne, and unto the Lamb for ever and ever."

XII

JEREMIAH—THE MAN WHO LOOKED LIKE CHRIST

"And others, Jeremiah."

MATTHEW 16:14

AT A CRISIS IN HIS MINISTRY JESUS WITHDREW with his disciples into the lonely region of Caesarea-Phillipi. There he asked his disciples, "Whom do men say that I the Son of man am?" The disciples answered him, "Some say that thou art John the Baptist; some Elijah; and others Jeremiah, or one of the prophets."

Christ was none of these with whom the popular thought associated him, and who were named by the disciples. Yet so far as a comparison, rather than a reincarnation, was concerned, those who said that Christ was Jeremiah were nearer to the truth than those who said he was John the Baptist, or those who said he was Elijah. John and Elijah had his zeal, his courage, his obedience to the will of God, his power to denounce; but only Jeremiah had his tenderness, his solitariness, his sorrow, his compassion, and his spiritual thought of the Kingdom of God. Isaiah's great portrait of the Suffering Servant of God in the fifty-third chapter of his prophecy,

JEREMIAH—WHO LOOKED LIKE CHRIST

which both Christ and the Evangelist Philip tell us was a prediction of Christ, was taken by some to be a portrait of the prophet Jeremiah. He indeed was "despised and rejected of men, a man of sorrows and acquainted with grief." It is by no means strange that some should have so misunderstood Isaiah, for it looks as if Jeremiah had sat for his portrait to Isaiah. Jeremiah is in many ways the saddest, loneliest, and grandest man in the Bible.

Nations produce their greatest men at the beginning of their history or at the end of their history, in the throes of birth or in the throes of dissolution. Jeremiah is the prophet of Israel's sunset. We behold him standing like an iron pillar amid the smoke and flames and darkness of Jerusalem's overthrow and destruction.

The span of his life covers one of the most dramatic and catastrophic periods of history. He was called in early manhood at his home at Anathoth to speak the Word of God to Judah and Jerusalem. He prophesied during the reign of Josiah and through the reign of Zedekiah, in all about forty-one years. Great world events occurred during this period. In 608 B.C., the good King Josiah was slain by Pharaoh Necho of Egypt. In 606 Babylon destroyed Nineveh and Assyria. In 605 Babylon under Nebuchadnezzar subjugated Egypt, and in 587 the temple was destroyed at Jerusalem, and shortly afterwards the people were carried into captivity. Thus in almost a quarter of a century two great empires, Assyria and Egypt, were destroyed; a new world empire, Babylon, rose to power; and Jerusalem was burned and its people carried into captivity. Treated kindly by the conqueror, Nebuchadnezzar, Jeremiah elected to remain at Jerusalem with the viceregent set up by Babylon, Gedaliah. But when this governor was murdered, the fugitives dragged the prophet with them down to Egypt, where he delivered his last predictions at Tahpanhes, and where, according to very ancient tradition, he was stoned to death. "They were stoned, they were sawn asunder."

To Jeremiah we owe some of the most beautiful, remarkable, brilliant, and striking passages of the Bible. Here are just a few of them:

"The harvest is past, the summer is ended, and we are not saved." (8:20)

"Peace, peace, when there is no peace." (6:14)

"Let not the wise man glory in his wisdom, neither let the mighty man glory in his might, let not the rich man glory in his riches; but let him that glorieth glory in this, that he understandeth and knoweth me." (9:23)

"The heart is deceitful above all things, and desperately wicked: who can know it?" (17:9)

"Is it nothing to you, all ye that pass by? behold and see if there be any sorrow like unto my sorrow." (Lam. 1:12)

JEREMIAH—WHO LOOKED LIKE CHRIST

"Can the Ethiopian change his skin, or the leopard his spots?" (13:23)

"Yea, I have loved thee with an everlasting love: therefore with loving-kindness have I drawn thee." (31:3)

"O earth, earth, earth, hear the word of the Lord." (22:29)

"Give glory to the Lord your God, before he cause darkness, and before your feet stumble upon the dark mountains." (13:16)

"I will put my law in their inward parts, and write it in their hearts; and will be their God, and they shall be my people. And they shall teach no more every man his neighbor, and every man his brother, saying, Know the Lord, for they shall all know me from the least of them unto the greatest of them, saith the Lord." (31:33, 34)

The message that Jeremiah was called to deliver he spoke with word and also with sign. With poetic imagination he imagines Rachel rising out of her tomb on the way to Bethlehem and weeping over her children as she sees them pass by on the long road to exile. Jeremiah was the greatest of the illustrative preachers. Now we see him going away down to the river Euphrates and digging up a girdle that he had been commanded to bury there, and bringing this marred girdle to Jerusalem to display to the people as a sign of the nation's corruption. And now we find him getting his sermon at the potter's house, where he asks his hearers to watch the potter as he takes a marred vessel and fashions it anew, for the clay is still soft and ductile; the symbol of what God could yet have done with Israel if the people had repented.

Another day we find him at the potter's house again; this time selecting a bottle that has been finished, baked, and hardened, which cannot now be changed or worked anew, and carrying it down into the dark valley of Hinnom, and there breaking it to pieces before the people, a symbol of the irrevocableness of Israel's doom and judgment. Again we see him bringing the Rechabites, whose ancient ancestors had pledged them to total abstinence, into the palace, and setting before them wine, which he knew they would refuse to drink. When they had refused to break the custom of their ancestors and drink the wine, Jeremiah used this as a sermon to contrast the fidelity of the Rechabites to the command of their ancestor with the infidelity of Jerusalem to the command and covenant of God. Another day we see him going up and down the streets of Jerusalem with a yoke on his shoulders, the yoke worn by the oxen in the fields, and on Jeremiah's shoulders the sign of Israel's subjugation. And even down in Egypt we see him hiding stones in the brickkiln at Tahpanhes, in the sight of the refugees from Israel, as a sign of the conquest of Egypt by Babylon.

JEREMIAH—WHO LOOKED LIKE CHRIST

Whether a spoken or an acted sermon, no one could misunderstand the meaning of his message.

Jeremiah was one of God's grandest prophets and witnesses. When Judas Maccabaeus was struggling for the religious liberty of the Jews and resisting the attempt of Antiochus to force idolatry upon the Hebrews, Jeremiah appeared to Judas and put in his hand a golden sword, saying, "Take this holy sword, a gift from God, with which thou shalt wound the adversaries." This story from the Apocrypha embodies the truth that Jeremiah, execrated, hated, and persecuted in his day and generation, became in later ages a watch cry and a symbol of victory to the people of Israel.

I

THE COURAGE AND FIDELITY OF JEREMIAH

Every great soul leaves to mankind a noble heritage. None left a nobler than did Jeremiah. As a servant of God and as a friend of man there are three things that mark and distinguish Jeremiah. The first is his courage. It fell to him during the years of the rise of Babylon as a world power and its increasing aggression on Jerusalem to speak a message of judgment upon the people of God for their sins and apostasies and to declare and predict the conquest of Jerusalem by Nebuchadnezzar, and the captivity of the people in Babylon.

This was why Jeremiah was the saddest and loneliest of men. He was a great lover of his city and of his people; yet he was commanded to foretell utter overthrow by Babylon and the captivity as a judgment upon the people for their sins. It is not strange, then, that Jeremiah suffered so much in spirit. Never did a national prophet and leader speak so hard and difficult a message. He felt himself an outcast, and like Job lamented the day he was born. Yet he never wavered in his loyalty to the Word of God. On one occasion he thought that he would cease to speak as God's prophet, but found that it was impossible. "Then I said I will not make mention of him nor speak any more in his name; but his word was in my heart, as a burning fire shut up in my bones, and I was weary with forbearing, and could not stay."

The position of Jeremiah as a prophet and national leader was in striking contrast with that of his great predecessor of a half century earlier, Isaiah. At that time Jerusalem was threatened by Assyria and Nebuchadnezzar, and Isaiah was given the commission to encourage the King Hezekiah in his resistance to the tyrant of Nineveh and to predict the utter overthrow of the armies of Sennacherib. But with Jeremiah it was altogether different. When Babylon was thundering at the gates of Jerusalem he had to proclaim the futility of resistance or of an alliance with Egypt, or with any other power, and foretell the ultimate fall and destruction of the city and the captivity of the people. We get some idea of his situation if we think of a preacher in England today standing in the pulpit of St. Paul's Cathedral and predicting the fall of London, the conquest of England by Germany, and the subjugation of Great Britain to Hitler. It is not strange, then, that the message of Jeremiah stirred up anger, rage, and persecution. He was hated, execrated, persecuted, derided, mocked, smitten, and cast into prison as a traitor and as an enemy of his people. Yet in all these perils he was delivered. The promise that God gave him when he called him to the prophet's office, "They shall fight against thee, but they shall not prevail against thee, for I am with thee, saith the Lord, to deliver thee," was gloriously fulfilled.

How grand a thing it was that God could count on him to the last degree, and how grand a thing it is that in every age God has prophets who will speak only the Word of the Lord. These are the men who have made humanity their debtor.

II

THE COMPASSION AND TENDERNESS OF JEREMIAH

The message of judgment and of woe and captivity was declared to Jerusalem by a man whose heart was tender and whose feelings were stirred within him. Well he could say, "I am the man that hath seen affliction." It was this that made him cry out, "O that I had in the wilderness a lodging place of way-faring men that I might leave my people and go from them." It was this that made him lament, "O that my head were waters, and mine eyes a fountain of tears, that I might weep day and night for the slain of the daughter of my people!" Truly he could say, identifying himself with the fate of Jerusalem, "Is it nothing to you, all ye that pass by? Behold, and see if there be any sorrow like unto my sorrow." Like all great souls, Jeremiah felt the sorrow and tragedy of a nation or a city, or a single soul, frustrating the grace of God and falling short of its destiny. Like every noble soul, he felt the sorrow and tragedy of the triumph of wickedness. As Christ wept over Jerusalem while he pronounced her destruction, so Jeremiah wept over Jerusalem as he spoke the words of her doom. We have not risen to Christlike standards or proportions until we can feel the sorrow and pathos of a nation departing from God, as our nation is doing today, or of a soul sinning against its Creator and denying its Redeemer, as so many souls are doing today.

III

JEREMIAH'S FAITH FOR THE FUTURE OF THE KINGDOM OF GOD

Shortly before the great prophet of Florence, Savonarola, was burned at the stake, he said, "If you ask me in general as to the issue of this trouble, I reply, Victory. If you ask me in a particular sense, I reply, Death; for the Master who wields the hammer, when he has used it, throws it away. So he did with Jeremiah, whom he caused to be stoned at the end of his ministry. But Rome will not put out this fire; and if this be put out, God will light another."

Likewise Jeremiah, while predicting the coming overthrow and destruction of Jerusalem, strikes the great note of God's restoration, and the kingdom of blessing and glory which will rise out of the ruins of the conquered city. God's purposes with Israel are not ended. He will make a full end of the nations to which he has driven them, but he will not make a full end of his people.

This faith in the future reaches its climax in his prediction of the New Covenant, the clearest and most spiritual of all the Old Testament prophecies of the Kingdom of Christ. "Behold the days come, saith the Lord, that I will make a new covenant with the house of Israel, and with the house of Judah. I will put my law in their inward parts, and write it in their hearts; and will be their God, and they shall be my people. And they shall teach no more every man his neighbor, and every man his brother, saying, Know the Lord: for they shall all know me, from the least of them unto the greatest of them, saith the Lord: for I will forgive their iniquity, and I will remember their sin no more."

Thus the prophet of doom becomes the prophet of hope. Jeremiah's sad face is illuminated, lighted, transfigured with the light of the glory of Christ. All who strive to do God's will in the world must pray that they may have the faith to see and to believe, even in the darkest day, what Jeremiah saw, the glory of the coming of the Lord.

The New Covenant was made by Christ and sealed with his blood. "This cup," he said, on the same night on which he was betrayed, "is the new covenant in my blood, which is shed for many for the remission of sins." All that God promises to do for his world, all that he promises to do for the salvation of our souls, is upon the ground of that new covenant that he made with man in Christ. The covenant stands forever. As God said to Jeremiah, "While stands my covenant with the day and the night, my covenant with man will stand." By that covenant we are admitted and restored to the family of God.

JEREMIAH—WHO LOOKED LIKE CHRIST

Would that I had Jeremiah's tenderness and compassion and faith and eloquence, as I now urge upon you to receive from God the blessings of the new covenant, the forgiveness of sins, the joy of fellowship with Christ, and the gift of Eternal Life.

XIII

DANIEL—THE MAN WHO LIVES FOREVER BECAUSE HE SAID NO

> "Daniel purposed in his heart that he would not defile himself with the portion of the king's meat."
>
> DANIEL 1:8

AN ORIENTAL KING ONCE SUMMONED INTO HIS presence his three sons and set before them three sealed urns, one of gold, one of amber, and the third of clay. The king bade his eldest son to choose among these three urns that which appeared to him to contain the greatest treasures. The eldest son chose the vessel of gold on which was written the word, "Empire." He opened it and found it full of blood. The second chose the vase of amber whereon was written the word, "Glory," and when he opened it he found it full of the ashes of men who had made a great name in the world. The third chose the vessel of clay, and on the bottom of this vessel was inscribed the name of God. The wise men at the king's court voted that the third vessel weighed the most because a single letter of the name of God weighed more than all the rest of the universe.

Daniel is one of those men who chose God above all else in the world. He lives forever because he said "No." Many of the greatest men of the Bible

DANIEL—WHO LIVES BECAUSE HE SAID NO

teach us and guide us, not only by their virtues, but by their transgressions. Noah, Abraham, David, and Peter were all great men, but men who had serious blemishes in their characters and dark chapters of unworthy conduct. But Daniel is one of those men in the Bible whose whole life, so far as we know their life, spoke on the side of righteousness and of truth. He is spoken of by the angel as "a man greatly beloved," and no doubt one of the reasons was that his long life was one of unbroken obedience to God and loyalty to the truth.

The different states of our country every year select young men from the universities of strong physique, superior intellect, and high character to be sent to Oxford University as Rhodes' scholars and drink at that fountain of culture and wisdom. The potentate of ancient Babylon, Nebuchadnezzar, was not indifferent to the advantages which it would bring to his kingdom to have choice young men from foreign lands brought up at Babylon in all the wisdom and statesmanship of his empire and trained for future service.

Therefore, Nebuchadnezzar after he took Jerusalem gave orders to his ministers to select among the inhabitants of Jerusalem four young men to be trained at Babylon. These young men were to be strong and without blemish in their bodies, of superior intellect, of strong character, and with qualities which would fit them to serve the Babylonian kingdom. The four young men selected were Daniel, Hananiah, Mishael, and Azariah—the three latter best known, however, by the Babylonian names that Nebuchadnezzar gave them, Shadrach, Meshach, and Abed-nego. You can imagine the great interest those young men took in the long journey from captive and wasted Jerusalem down into Mesopotamia —how they wondered at the desert which they crossed, and then the tawny flood of the Euphrates, and then the great city of Babylon, an immense pile of bricks and mud, and most of all at the palace of Nebuchadnezzar, and the royal park with the hanging gardens which the king had built for his queen who in the flat country around Babylon was homesick for her native hills and mountains.

The young men were quartered in the king's palace and were to sit at the king's table and eat of the food and drink the wine which was served to the royal family. This precipitated the difficulty and the crisis in the life of Daniel and these three young men. All that the king of Baylon ate or drank had been blessed by being offered before heathen idols, and among the articles of diet, too, were things which no Hebrew by the law of Moses was permitted to eat. Today we do not think much of that particular kind of defilement, for Jesus taught that it is not what goes into a man that defiles him, but

DANIEL—WHO LIVES BECAUSE HE SAID NO

what comes out of his heart. But at that time for a Jew to eat what had been offered to a heathen idol, or to eat meat that was forbidden by the Jewish law, was to defile himself and to renounce his faith and his God.

This, then, was the crisis which confronted Daniel and his three companions. To drink or not to drink? To eat, or not to eat? Everything, so far as the world was concerned, so far as external things, material things, were concerned, was of a nature to lead Daniel to submit to the diet that was prescribed for him. In the first place it appealed to the appetite of the body. Nebuchadnezzar's wine was the best wine in the world. It made the heart glad and the eye sparkle. The meats and dainties which were served represented the highest skill of the culinary art. There were brains of peacocks, pheasants from the forests of Armenia, rare birds from India, rare fish from distant seas, and the savory flesh of swine from the royal herd fed on acorns.

Again, Daniel was far from home; and save for these three companions, who would do just as he did, he was unobserved by any one of his own race and faith. Jerusalem had fallen. The Hebrew monarchy was coming to an end. If Daniel had a future that future must be in Babylon. He might have said to himself, "In Babylon let us do as the Babylonians do." Moreover, not to eat of the things served at the king's table would invite the ridicule and the derision of other young men from other countries who had been brought to Babylon for the same purposes as Daniel. They would point the finger of scorn at these Hebrews who would not drink the king's wine or eat the king's meat. By doing just as others did, going along with the rest of these graduate students, Daniel and his friends would escape the finger of scorn and mockery. Then, too, not to submit to the diet prescribed by the king would, under ordinary circumstances, provoke the king to wrath. Such a refusal would imperil Daniel's future. It might be a barrier to his progress and to his promotion to high place in the kingdom. And still more, it might mean his death.

But all these considerations moved Daniel not at all. He chose God. "Daniel purposed in his heart that he would not defile himself with the portion of the king's meat." The grandest thing that the sun that day looked down on in Babylon, the most royal bit of furniture about the court of Nebuchadnezzar, the noblest creature in God's universe, was a man with a moral purpose, an immortal soul, taking this quiet stand for righteousness, with time, circumstance, expediency, the appetites of the flesh, the chances of promotion, the will of the potentate of the whole earth, personal safety, all leading and urging in the other direction; and yet overcoming all these

DANIEL—WHO LIVES BECAUSE HE SAID NO

influences was a moral purpose, and a decision of soul.

I

THE MORAL COURAGE OF DANIEL WON RESPECT EVEN FROM A PAGAN COURT

God gave Daniel favor with the king's chamberlain. Instead of reporting him to the king as an impudent upstart who ought to be expelled or executed, he said that even at the risk of endangering his own head he would exempt Daniel and his companions from the course prescribed by the king and permit them to experiment with their own Hebrew fare, which consisted of pulse, or beans, and water. The dietitians of our own day bear witness to the nourishing qualities of such a fare.

Although on the surface the world may appear to scorn and ridicule the man who has the courage to differ from its fashion and custom, in their hearts even worldly men honor and respect moral courage. No one ever lost anything even from the standpoint of this world by taking a stand for principle. Who would disown his family? Who would disown his friends? Who would disown his country? Why, then, fear to be loyal to that which is above country, and friends, and family, the soul's invisible and spiritual companions and friends, those holy convictions, those pure aspirations, those righteous determinations which alone make men great?

II

DANIEL'S "NO" INFLUENCED OTHERS AND GAVE THEM COURAGE TO SAY "NO"

Nothing is said of it here directly, but it is plain that by announcing his determination not to defile himself with the king's meat, Daniel gave encouragement and strength to his three companions so that they too said "No." We can tell that from the subsequent trial to which Shadrach, Meshach, and Abed-nego were subjected. For some reason unknown to us Daniel was exempted from this trial; but the three young men were commanded to bow down and worship the image of Nebuchadnezzar as soon as they heard the royal orchestra strike up its music; and if they would not, they were to be cast into the fiery furnace. The three young men then gave their magnificent answer. They said they would not bow down and worship the king's image. They believed that the God of Israel would deliver them. But even if he did not, even if it was the will of God that they should perish in the fiery furnace, still they would not bow down. And they did not bow down. And although they were cast into the fiery furnace the flames did not burn them;

and when the officers of Nebuchadnezzar came to look upon this wonder, the three men standing unhurt in the midst of the furnace, they saw standing with them a fourth figure, one like unto the Son of Man himself. Who inspired that great stand made by those three Hebrew lads? I am sure it was Daniel, who, when the first temptation was set before him and his companions in Babylon, said "No," and purposed in his heart that he would not defile himself. You can never tell when your refusal, your "No," is going to show the way and give heart and strength to some other to take the right way; and you never know when your consent, or your weakness, or your acquiescence is going to lead some other soul astray and start him on that path that goes down into darkness.

> "Oh, strengthen me that while I stand
> Firm on the rock and strong in thee,
> I may stretch out a loving hand
> To wrestlers with the angry sea." [1]

III

DANIEL MADE THIS DECISION WHEN HE WAS FIRST CONFRONTED WITH THE TEMPTATION

Here these four young men are sitting in their

---

[1] Francis R. Havergal.

chambers on that first night in the king's palace at Babylon. They have been dressed and made ready for the royal table by the servants. The first gong for dinner has sounded. One of the waiters has brought them up a menu. They see at once that most of the articles are foods forbidden by the Jewish law. So they sit down to talk it over. What shall we do? Suppose Shadrach had said, "Perhaps we had better go along tonight. Let the matter rest for a little. It may be that by getting the favor of the king's chamberlain, after a few days, or after a week or two, we can persuade him to exempt us from this diet. But to stand out and say 'No' on the first night, at the very start, is likely to get us into trouble." Suppose they had agreed to that policy? Then all of them would have been lost, so far as their loyalty to Israel and God was concerned, and the world would never have been thrilled, as it has been from age to age, with the story of how those three Hebrew lads went into the fiery furnace rather than bow down to the image of Nebuchadnezzar, and how Daniel, the Hebrew statesman, opened his window towards Jerusalem and was cast into the den of lions rather than pray to King Darius.

The time to get the advantage of temptation is when it first appears. To parley with it, to postpone a decision with regard to it, is almost always fatal to the soul.

DANIEL—WHO LIVES BECAUSE HE SAID NO

It is plain from the record that even before the matter of the forbidden diet had been brought before Daniel he had come down to Babylon determined to be true to God. Therefore, it was not difficult for him to say "No" when this particular temptation arose. He had already committed himself to right principles and to loyalty to God. It was written of one of the kings of Israel, Rehoboam, that "he did evil because he had not prepared his heart to seek the Lord." There you have the secret of the moral breakdown of many persons. They succumb to evil because they have never really purposed in their hearts to resist it. They do evil because they have never set themselves to do good. You may wish to live the right life, you may have a general desire to be true and clean and courageous and Christlike; but that in itself is not sufficient. You must not only wish but *will* to do the right. Satan is always trying to sift a man as he tried to sift Peter, and as he tried to sift Daniel. And he generally succeeds in doing so when he encounters a soul which has not set itself against evil and determined in the heart not to defile itself. People like to make a wish when they see the stars in a certain conjunction, or when they stand by a wishing well, or on a wishing stairway, or when they pull the wishbone of a fowl. But the men who succeed in life, the men who stand the battering of

Satan, are those who depend, not upon the wishbone, but upon the backbone.

IV

DANIEL PURPOSED THAT HE WOULD NOT DEFILE HIMSELF

Mark that. He would not defile himself. That means that Daniel was convinced that there was something sacred and godlike within him, and that it was worth every sacrifice and every danger, and even life itself, to keep that sacredness within him from being defiled. If you have the high Christian view of yourself, of your soul, as a beautiful and sacred thing, so sacred that even the Son of God died to redeem it, then the power of temptation is broken.

In a great passage, one of the noblest in English prose, and one of the most inspiring for young men, John Milton said that he was kept back from the vices and immoralities which stained the lives of his fellow students at Christ College, Cambridge, because he had "a just and pious reverence for his own person." In another passage he gives two reasons why a man ought not to sin against God and against himself. The first is the dignity of God's image upon him by creation, and the second the price of his redemption. "He thinks himself both a fit person to do the noblest and goodliest deeds, and much better worth than to defile with such a debasement and pollution as sin is, himself, so highly ransomed and ennobled to a new friendship and filial relation with God."

How splendidly that puts it! You have not only been created in the image of God, but been highly ransomed and ennobled to a new friendship with God by the death of Christ for you on the cross. Daniel purposed not to defile himself with the king's meat because he realized that there was a sacred soul within him. You have a great advantage over Daniel. You know not only what he knew, that you have been created in the image of God, but also what Daniel could not know, that you have been redeemed and ransomed by the precious blood of Christ. If you are worth that to God, then what ought you not to do for yourself?

XIV

JOSHUA—THE MAN AFTER WHOM JESUS WAS NAMED

> "Joshua the son of Nun, the servant of the Lord."
>
> JOSHUA 24:29

"THE SERVANT OF THE LORD." THAT IS ONE OF the greatest epitaphs of the Bible. It was spoken of Moses, one of the greatest men in the Bible, when he died "on Nebo's lonely mountain"; and here it is spoken of Joshua at the end of his great and heroic life. "Joshua the servant of the Lord." That always, and pre-eminently, he was. No man ever lived who more deserved that epitaph.

At first it may seem strange that when our Saviour, the Son of God, came into the world he was given for his personal name the name of Joshua, the greatest warrior of the Old Testament. Why not Moses, or Samuel, or Elijah, or even David, or Isaiah? But the angel told Joseph before the birth of Mary's child that he was to call his name Jesus, which is the New Testament form of Joshua, and which means "The Lord is salvation," and in connection with Christ meant that he would save his people from their sins. In certain great aspects Jesus, the Prince of Peace, who shed no blood but

JOSHUA—AFTER WHOM JESUS WAS NAMED

his own, and Joshua, the blood-stained conqueror of Canaan, are much alike. Both did wholly the will of God. It was said of Joshua that he left nothing undone, of all that the Lord commanded Moses; and on the cross Jesus cried out, "It is finished." Joshua foreshadows Christ in his complete obedience to the will of God; and as Joshua led the people across the River Jordan and conquered Canaan for them, so Jesus by the power of his death and resurrection leads his people through the Jordan of death and into the Promised Land of peace and rest. It was said of Joshua at the end of his great life that he gave the people "rest," and so Christ has prepared rest from the toil and trouble and sorrow and sin of this world for his people.

> "There is a land of pure delight,
>   Where saints immortal reign;
> Infinite day excludes the night,
>   And pleasures banish pain.
>
> "Sweet fields beyond the swelling flood
>   Stand dressed in living green;
> So to the Jews old Canaan stood,
>   While Jordan rolled between."[1]

There is therefore more than an accidental similarity, but rather a deep significance and association

---

[1] Isaac Watts.

in these two names, the Joshua of the Old Testament and the Joshua and Jesus of the New Testament.

I

THE COURAGE OF JOSHUA

Joshua is the Great Heart of the Old Testament. The first appearance of Joshua on the great stage of Israel's history was when he commanded the battle against the Amalekites at Rephidim. In that critical battle, when the Amalekites withstood the Israelites as they entered the peninsula of Sinai, Joshua did the fighting, while Moses, his weary hands upheld by Aaron and Hur, did the praying on the hilltop. Of all the men in Israel, it was Joshua who was chosen by Moses to lead the battle against the Amalekites.

The next appearance of Joshua was when he went up with the twelve spies to spy out the land. When they returned from their survey of Canaan after a forty days' journey, the spies brought back as a sample of the fruitfulnes of the land a cluster of grapes, so large that it had to be carried on the shoulders of two men. All agreed, too, that it was a fruitful and productive land, one that flowed with milk and honey. But ten of the spies advised against attempting to conquer the land. They said it was a land that "ate up all the inhabitants thereof," and that all the people that they saw there were giants

JOSHUA—AFTER WHOM JESUS WAS NAMED

and sons of the giants, and that in their sight the twelve Hebrew spies were but grasshoppers.

When the congregation heard this, they lifted up their voices and murmured against Moses, and said, "Let us make a captain, and let us return unto Egypt." But two of the spies, Caleb and Joshua, dissented from the majority, declaring that if they went up at once and fought for it, they could conquer the land, and that it was well worth fighting for. So enraged were the people at this favorable report, and so broken had their spirit been by the report of the ten spies, that they took up stones to stone Joshua and Caleb. But before they could carry out their purpose, the glory of the Lord appeared at the tabernacle and God sentenced the people to the forty years of wandering in the desert because of their lack of faith and lack of courage. Of all the host who were adults when they left Egypt, only two, Joshua and Caleb, were permitted to see the Promised Land and enter into it. Joshua belonged to a noble minority.

> "Minorities, since time began—
> Have shown the better side of man.
> And often in the lists of time
> One man has made a cause sublime." [2]

The inferiority, the grasshopper complex, still

---
[2] Paul Lawrence Dunbar.

prevails. Whenever a great work is to be done, a forward step taken, or an attack made upon an entrenched iniquity, about ten out of twelve are timid and afraid, and see themselves as grasshoppers in the presence of the difficulty to be overcome and the great enemies to be conquered. Only about two out of twelve are strong enough and bold enough to march forward in the name of the Lord. The favorite refrain of the book of Joshua is this, "Be strong and of a good courage." Over and over again that word is spoken to Joshua and by him to the people. The courage of Joshua was the high and invincible courage that is founded upon faith. When you have faith in the success of a cause you are not afraid and not ashamed to fight for it. The enemies which oppose the people of God today are not less numerous and not less strongly entrenched than were those tribes which Joshua drove out of the land of Canaan. What is needed is men who are baptized with the courage of Joshua, a courage that is born of unfaltering faith in God and his Word.

II

JOSHUA AS A MAN OF DEVOTION

We think of Joshua as the leader on the field of battle. But we must remember that he was schooled for his great task in a very particular way by fellow-

JOSHUA—AFTER WHOM JESUS WAS NAMED

ship with the Divine. He was taken by Moses to Mount Sinai, and was in attendance upon Moses as his minister when he wrote the law on the tables of stone. There he heard and saw the majesty of God. But more striking still was the appearance of the Angel of the Lord to Joshua as he commenced the conquest of Canaan. It was just after they had passed over Jordan, and before the attack was made on Jericho. Joshua was reconnoitering that city, when he beheld a man over against him, with his sword in his hand. In his bluff, soldierly fashion Joshua went up to him and said in accents which admitted of no neutrality, "Art thou for us, or for our adversaries?" And the mysterious man answered, "Nay, but as captain of the host of the Lord am I now come." When Joshua heard this he fell on his face to the earth and worshiped. Joshua fought his battles, henceforth, with a sword that was "bathed in heaven." Back of his heroic achievements was a deep acquaintance with the holiness and the majesty of God. It cannot be otherwise with us in the battle of life. There must be Sinai, mountain-top experiences, quiet nocturnal meetings with God, meetings which declare the eternal reality of the spiritual world and which pronounce the certain victory of truth and righteousness.

III

JOSHUA BUILT FOR THE FUTURE

One of the noblest things about this titanic man is his noble thought for tomorrow, his desire for the generation which was to follow him. He had a passion for righteousness in Israel, not only the Israel of today, but the Israel of tomorrow. When he realized that his own race was nearly run and that he had fought his last battle, he called for the leaders of the people, and telling them that he was going the way of all the earth, exhorted them to hold fast to their faith in God. The approaching sunset of his own life in no respect diminished his faith or his zeal for God. "Cleave unto the Lord your God," he said, "for the Lord your God, he it is that fighteth for you, as he hath promised you."

To plan for the future, to think of those who come after us, whether it be planting a tree which shall give its shade to some weary one on the pilgrimage of life, long after our own pilgrimage is over, to plan that our money shall serve some great and Christian end when we can no longer spend it, to instill into our children principles of faith and of manhood which shall strengthen them and guide them when our own warfare is long over, this is always the mark of the highest faith and the noblest courage.

JOSHUA—AFTER WHOM JESUS WAS NAMED

"An old man going a lone highway
Came at the evening cold and gray
To a chasm vast and deep and wide.
The old man crossed in the twilight dim,
The sullen stream had no fear for him,
But he stopped when safe on the other side
And builded a bridge to stem the tide.

" 'Old Man,' said a fellow pilgrim near,
'You are wasting your strength with building here;
Your journey will end with the ending day,
You never again will pass this way,
You've crossed the chasm deep and wide,
Why build you this bridge at eventide?'

"The builder lifted his old gray head,
'Good friend, in the path I have come,' he said,
'There followeth after me today
A youth whose feet must pass this way.
This chasm which has been as naught to me
To that fair-haired youth might a pitfall be,
He, too, must cross in the twilight dim,
Good friend, I am building this bridge for him.' " [3]

IV

JOSHUA, A MAN OF DECISION

Joshua was a man of decision. There is never any wavering, faltering, hesitating, or delaying, when the way of duty has been made clear to him. He had

---

[3] Will Allen Dromgoole.

decided for the God of Israel, and the deeds of every day of his life rang with that decision.

Not only did he choose God for himself, but he called upon others to choose God. In one of the great scenes of the Bible he assembled the people at Shechem, all the tribes and all their leaders, and told them what great things God had done for Israel in the past, and then called on them to decide whether they were going to serve the Lord, or serve the gods of the people on the other side of the Jordan, or the gods of the Amorites in the land of Canaan. "Choose ye this day whom ye will serve!"

The world needs men who can preach like Joshua; not only rehearse and describe the great things of God and of Christ, but persuade men to choose them, and to choose them *now*. "Choose ye this day whom ye will serve." How much real indecision, how much suspended allegiance, how much halting between two opinions there is in any assembly like this! Whom will ye serve? Joshua told the people that they could have a wide selection of gods to choose from, if they did not want to serve the God of Israel. They could worship the gods of the Amorites, or the gods of any of the tribes and peoples who lived on the other side of the Jordan. There are plenty of gods whom you can serve, aside from the true God and his Son Jesus Christ. Among these gods are

JOSHUA—AFTER WHOM JESUS WAS NAMED

business, society, money, power, fame, appetite, pleasure. But what are all these gods compared with Jesus Christ? What Christ has done, what God has done for those who believed in him and followed him and chose him for time and for eternity is indelibly written on the pages of the past. Who ever chose God and lived to regret that choice? Some one of the gods of this world, some one of its fading pleasures and dwindling satisfactions will have the service and energy of your life, if you do not give it to God and to Christ. Why not choose, and choose now, to serve God? Then at the end yours too shall be that glorious epitaph of Joshua, *"the servant of the Lord."*

XV

JOB—THE MAN WHO MADE SATAN QUIT

> "We count them happy which endure. Ye have heard of the patience of Job."
>
> JAMES 5:11

YES, JAMES, WE HAVE ALL HEARD OF THE PATIENCE of Job, not only those to whom you were writing, but those to whom I am now speaking. Age after age, generation after generation has heard of the endurance of Job and has wondered at it. Man is born to trouble as the sparks fly upward, and from the battle of life he can have no discharge. But among all the strugglers, battlers, sufferers, Job is the supreme example of the man who, in spite of his troubles, and in spite of his doubts, holds fast to God, and in the end sees the vindication of his faith.

Everybody ought to read at least one great book before he dies and enters into the presence of the Truth himself. There are many great books; but the consensus of human opinion seems to be that the Book of Job is the greatest of all. When you take up Job; Shakespeare, Milton, Plato, Homer can all go out of the window. In Carlyle's beautiful tribute in *Heroes and Hero Worship,* "Here in this book is sublime sorrow, sublime reconciliation, oldest choral

JOB—THE MAN WHO MADE SATAN QUIT

melody, as of the heart of mankind, so soft and great as the summer midnight, as the world with its seas and stars."

Who was Job? Nobody knows. When did he live? Nobody knows. What was his race? Nobody knows. Where did he live? Where was the land of Uz? No one knows. And this is all the better for the purpose of the great book because it makes Job a universal man, a representative of all mankind in his relationship to the world and to God.

More profound treatises have been written on the Book of Job than upon any other book of the Bible, and many of these books on Job may be described in the language of that sublime book itself, "Who is this that darkeneth counsel by words without knowledge?" Many of these books are so profound that they are obscure. Yet the message of this great book, although profound, taking hold upon the deep realities of life, is nevertheless simple. As deepest waters are clearest, so is the message of this book.

Now let us turn to the story of Job, but always remembering that it is easier to talk of Job than to bear what he had to bear, or to act like Job.

"There was a man in the land of Uz, whose name was Job, and that man was perfect and upright, and one that feared God and eschewed evil." John prayed for his friend Gaius that he might prosper and be in health even as his soul prospered. Job was a man who answered that description. He was a good man and had prosperity of soul. With that prosperity of soul there went good health and prosperity in worldly things. He had seven sons and three daughters. The thousands of his sheep whitened the face of the desert. Five hundred yoke of oxen and five hundred she-asses ploughed his fields for him, and three thousand camels transported his products to the markets of the world. He was the greatest of all the men of the east, but in his prosperity he never forgot God. He tells us later, when he is pouring out his soul in agony, that even in the midst of his prosperity he had realized that it might not last. When his sons and daughters feasted in their homes the pious Job rose up early and prayed for them, as many a devout father and mother has done since; "for," he said, "it may be that my sons have sinned and cursed God in their hearts."

The next scene introduces us to a council in heaven. All the sons of God come to present themselves before God, and among them Satan, the fallen angel, and now man's adversary. God says to Satan, "Whence comest thou?" "From going to and fro in the earth and from walking up and down in it," is Satan's answer. Then the Lord said to Satan, "Hast thou considered my servant Job, that there is

JOB—THE MAN WHO MADE SATAN QUIT

none like him in the earth, a perfect and an upright man, one that feareth God, and escheweth evil?"

At this description of Job, whom he knew well, for Satan knows us all, Satan answered with a sneer, "Doth Job fear God for nought? Hast thou not made an hedge about him, and about his house, and about all that he hath on every side? Thou hast blessed the work of his hands, and his substance is increased in the land. But put forth thine hand now and touch all that he hath, and he will curse thee to thy face."

It was as if Satan had said to the Lord, "Look at Job's prosperity; but take away his flocks and herds, his possessions and his family, and it will be a different story." Satan here advances the principle that there is no disinterested worship or faith, and that no man will serve God or believe in him for nought. It is important for the world and the ages to know that there is such faith, and that apparently is the great purpose of the book, to show us a man who will serve God for nought. Job did not know that he was being tested for that purpose, but that was the high purpose of the book. God may wish to demonstrate to the world some principle of faith and of Christian light in your life and in mine even as he did in the life of Job.

In the case of Job, God accepts Satan's challenge,

and tells him to go out and touch all that he has; only upon himself he is not to put his hand.

I

THE FIRST TEST

Then comes the first test. A messenger comes to Job and tells him that as the oxen were plowing and the asses feeding beside them, a band of Sabeans fell upon them and drove them off and slew all his servants except the teller of the bad tidings. That was bad news indeed, for the oxen and the asses were necessary for the cultivation of Job's extensive domains. But he remembered his thousands of sheep and camels, and, no doubt, said to himself, "I have still much left and much to be thankful for." Then came a second blow. Fire fell from heaven and burned up the sheep and the shepherds. That, too, was bad, for the sheep represented one of Job's chief sources of prosperity. But he thought of his camels. They were worth a great deal of money, and with them for capital he could purchase more sheep and more oxen to replace those that had perished.

But while he was thinking on this a third messenger came and told that a band of Chaldeans had made a raid and driven off all his camels. That, indeed, was bad. All Job's worldly possessions were gone, and all in one day. But Job remembered his family. He still had left his seven sons and three daughters. They would care for him in his adversity, and help him to start life over again. But while he thought on this a fourth messenger came and brought him the worst news of all. A whirlwind had smitten the house of his eldest son, where his sons and daughters were eating and drinking, and it fell upon them and buried all his children in the ruins.

When Job heard this, the climax of his calamity, his oxen and asses gone, his sheep gone, his camels gone, his children gone, he rent his mantle and fell down in his sorrow and distress on the ground. Yet he did not do what Satan said he would do under the circumstances. He did not curse or renounce God, but bowed before the will of God, and said, what has been said in circumstances of sorrow and distress ever since, "Naked came I out of my mother's womb, and naked shall I return thither: the Lord gave and the Lord hath taken away; blessed be the name of the Lord."

Job had withstood Satan's first assault. He had proved that he did not serve God for nought, and that stripped of all his possessions and all his children, he still believed in God.

Now comes the second conclave in heaven. The sons of God again present themselves before him, and among them Satan. God again asks Satan about Job, the good man who held fast his integrity, although without cause Satan had moved God to permit him to try him. But Satan is not yet convinced that Job is impregnable in his faith. He answers God: "Skin for skin, yea all that a man hath will he give for his life. Put forth thine hand now and touch his bone and his flesh and he will curse thee to thy face." It was as if Satan had said to the Lord, "Job still holds to his faith, although he has lost his possessions and his family. But take away his health from him, leave him in pain and agony of body, and he will no longer believe."

II

THE SECOND TEST

Again Satan gets permission to stretch forth his hand and touch Job's body, but with this limitation, he is not to take his life. And that limitation was the mystery to Job when the blow fell upon him. Why did not God, who brought such suffering upon him, end his life? But if God had permitted Satan to do that, there could have been no demonstration of faith in God.

The second test of Job's integrity and faith is this physical and personal one. Job was smitten with sore boils from the sole of his foot unto the crown of his head. It was some loathsome, painful, disgusting disease that made him impossible for all those around him; and seeing that, realizing it, Job left his house and went out to the outskirts of the city and sat on the dung heap that always lifted its dismal pile near the oriental city; and there in his misery, sitting amid the ashes of the burnt offal, Job scraped himself with a potsherd.

His own wife, perhaps out of an ungenerous heart, perhaps out of sympathy with his terrible distress, advised him to curse God and die. In view of the terrible calamities which had fallen upon Job, his wife evidently felt that for him longer to pretend to believe in God was preposterous. But Job still holds fast. "What," he said to his wife, "shall we receive good at the hand of God and shall we not receive evil?"

III

THE THREE FRIENDS

Satan's second assault upon Job has failed. Now Satan fades out of the drama, and Job's three friends come to mourn with him and comfort him. These three friends, Eliphaz, Bildad, and Zophar, however wrong in many respects their theology, are to be commended for the sympathy which brought them from afar to sit near Job as he scraped himself on his dunghill. So wretched was Job's condition, so terrific the change that had come over him, that his three friends did not know him, and could not recognize in him their old friend, the great emir, the greatest man of all the east.

For seven days they sat near him in silence, never speaking, for "they saw that his grief was great." Sometimes the most eloquent speech is the silence of compassion. At the end of those seven days Job breaks down. He does not curse God, but he does, by implication, question and condemn the providence of God in his life, for in one of the most eloquent passages of this most eloquent of all books, Job curses the day he was born. That most mysterious of all human words, Why? is now upon the lips of Job, as it has been upon the lips of many another since Job. Job wants the day that he was born expunged from the calendar. "Why died I not from the womb?" He regrets that he had ever been called into being, and longs as many another sufferer has longed, for the deep silence of the grave, where the wicked cease from troubling and the weary are at rest. Why is light given to man whose way is hid? Why does God not let him die?

The three friends of Job now begin to speak. Three times, each one in order addresses Job, and three times Job, and frequently with mockery and defiance, answers them and pours out the agony of his soul. At first his friends deal gently with him.

JOB—THE MAN WHO MADE SATAN QUIT

They express their surprise that one who had been so noted for his faith and had strengthened others in their faith, has broken down in this way and found the consolations of God small with him. "Behold," they said, "thou hast instructed many. Thy words have upholden him that was falling . . . . but now it is come upon thee and thou faintest; it toucheth thee, and thou art troubled."

As Job continues to answer them, to defend his integrity, to pour out his agonizing questions to God, his friends grow angry with him. Their fundamental proposition is that all suffering is the result of sin, and that since Job has suffered so terribly, his sin must be exceedingly great. They even go the length of saying that since Job, before calamity had come upon him, had such a reputation for piety and faith, he must not only be a great sinner, but the worst kind of a sinner, a great hypocrite.

Job flings their charges back in their faces, and then turns in pathetic appeal to God. He would plead his case with God. He would come before God and speak with him. But where is God? He cannot find him. "O that I knew where I might find him, that I might come even to his seat! Behold I go forward, but he is not there; and backward, but I cannot perceive him; on the left hand where he doth work, but I cannot behold him; he hideth himself on the right hand that I cannot see him."

Now and then in the midst of his lamentation and agony he strikes the note of a great hope of life and vindication after death. "For I know that my Redeemer liveth, and that he shall stand at the latter day upon the earth, and though after my skin worms destroy this body, yet in my flesh shall I see God."

Though Job questions God, and even arraigns his providence and his justice in his life, the thing to remember is that he never curses God, never renounces him. Always he is stretching out his hands to find him. The creed of his agony, the agony of a good conscience, the creed of his dunghill is this, "Though he slay me yet will I trust."

Despairing of defeating Job in their arguments, the three friends at length are silent. Then a fourth man begins to speak, the eloquent Elihu, who has sat as a listener to the long and tempestuous debate. Elihu rebukes the three friends because they had not been able to silence Job and because many of their arguments were not true; but he also rebukes Job for his self-righteousness and exhorts him to humility and repentance. He reminds him of the greatness of God and the littleness of man. In this respect the speech of Elihu prepares the way for the next great act in this drama, the speech of God himself.

IV

GOD'S ANSWER

God answers Job out of the whirlwind. But what a strange answer, at first, it seems. There is no explanation of why Job had lost his camels, and his sheep, and his oxen, and his family, or why he had been so fearfully afflicted in his body. No answer as to why he had been born. No answer as to why he was not permitted now to die. Job has asked questions. Now God answers him with more questions. These questions have to do with the majesty of God as the Creator and Ruler of the Universe. "Where wast thou when I laid the foundations of the earth, ... when the morning stars sang together and all the sons of God shouted for joy? .... Hast thou commanded the morning and caused the day spring to know his place? .... Where is the way where light dwelleth? Canst thou bind the sweet influence of Pleiades, or loose the bands of Orion?"

And thus, in passages of overwhelming beauty and sublimity, God reveals his greatness in the universe, and exposes to Job the limitations of his knowledge. Job at length sees the point of it all. He understands that if he can know so little about God in creation, in the world, it is not strange that he cannot understand him in his providence, in his dealings with Job in his own life. Overcome by the manifestation of God's glory, Job humbles himself and repents. "I have heard of thee by the hearing of the ear; but now my eye seeth thee; wherefore I abhor myself, and repent in dust and ashes." Of what did Job repent? Not of any of those sins which his friends had falsely charged against him. He repented of his lack of faith, of his lack of submission, of his lack of humbling himself under the hand of God.

When Job repents he is restored to his old estate. He prays for his friends who had spoken unjustly of him and falsely of God and his ways. Then God turned the captivity of Job. All his friends and acquaintances came from afar and made their contributions to his material welfare so that he could start life over again. Seven sons and three beautiful daughters took the place of those he had lost, and Job is again the great man of the east. "So Job died, being old and full of days."

V

WHAT JOB TELLS US

Such is the world's greatest book. And what does it say to you and me? It tells us, in the first place, of the certainty of trial, of the certainty of our separation from those things which constitute worldly happiness. God will find out in us, as he did in

JOB—THE MAN WHO MADE SATAN QUIT

Job, whether or not we serve God for nought. Can we stand his test and search and come forth pure gold as Job did?

The great book tells us again that God is too great to be explained, to be discussed, to be analyzed, to be complained against by man. God is to be obeyed and trusted, to be held to, even as Job said he would hold to him, "Though he slay me, yet will I trust him."

Again, the great book tells us of the purpose of God in our life, which is to produce and crown and reward spiritual and moral qualities. After all, practical, common-sense, unpoetical James gives us the most satisfactory, although the briefest, commentary on Job, when he says, "We count them happy which endure. Ye have heard of the endurance of Job, and have seen the end of the Lord, that the Lord is very pitiful and of tender mercy." Yes; that is what we see in the case of Job. We see "the end of the Lord." We see what he is working at. We see what purpose he had in mind. In this respect you and I have a great advantage over suffering Job. We not only have the knowledge of how at the end of his trial, because he held fast to God, God blessed him, but we have the sure teaching of our Christian faith that all things work together for good to them that love God.

In your hour of trial, remember Job. And remember "the end of the Lord," that the Lord, although so great and majestic, is very pitiful and of tender mercy. Wait, I say, on the Lord!

> "God moves in a mysterious way
> His wonders to perform;
> He plants his footsteps in the sea,
> And rides upon the storm.
>
> "Deep in unfathomable mines
> Of never-failing skill
> He treasures up his bright designs,
> And works his sovereign will.
>
> "Judge not the Lord by feeble sense,
> But trust him for his grace;
> Behind a frowning providence
> He hides a smiling face." [1]

---

[1] William Cowper.